From Jo'burg to Jozi

Ade
Welcome to one
of the most
complicated societies
on the planet!
Heidi
9/3/06

From Jo'burg to Jozi

Stories about Africa's infamous city

Heidi Holland

Edited by
Heidi Holland & Adam Roberts

PENGUIN BOOKS

PENGUIN BOOKS

Published by the Penguin Group
Penguin Books (South Africa) (Pty) Ltd, 24 Sturdee Avenue, Rosebank, Johannesburg
2196, South Africa
Penguin Books Ltd, 80 Strand, London WC2R 0RL, England
Penguin Group (USA) Inc, 375 Hudson Street, New York, New York 10014, USA
Penguin Group (Canada), 90 Eglinton Avenue East, Suite 700, Toronto, Ontario,
Canada M4P 2Y3 (a division of Pearson Penguin Canada Inc)
Penguin Ireland, 25 St Stephen's Green, Dublin 2, Ireland (a division of
Penguin Books Ltd)
Penguin Group (Australia), 250 Camberwell Road, Camberwell, Victoria 3124,
Australia (a division of Pearson Australia Group Pty Ltd)
Penguin Books India Pvt Ltd, 11 Community Centre, Panchsheel Park,
New Delhi – 110 017, India
Penguin Group (NZ), Cnr Rosedale and Airborne Roads, Albany, Auckland 1310, New
Zealand (a division of Pearson New Zealand Ltd)

Penguin Books (South Africa) (Pty) Ltd, Registered Offices:
24 Sturdee Avenue, Rosebank, Johannesburg 2196, South Africa

www.penguinbooks.co.za

First published by Penguin Books (South Africa) (Pty) Ltd 2002
Reprinted 2003, 2006

Selection Copyright © Heidi Holland & Adam Roberts 2002
Preface © Heidi Holland
Introduction © Adam Roberts
Individual contributions © The authors
The Acknowledgements on page 258 constitute an extension of this copyright notice
All rights reserved
The moral right of the authors and editors has been asserted

ISBN 0 143 02419 1

Typeset by CJH Design in 10.5/13pt Charter
Printed and bound by Interpak Books, Pietermaritzburg

For
Anne
with an e, pronounced with an a

Contents

Preface

The idea for this book began when Adam Roberts and I, both journalists, were discussing the subjects and structures we were proposing to tackle as authors. Adam was considering a book on Johannesburg, while I was thinking of exploring the short story form in a writing style other than journalese. We thought it would be interesting to write one thousand words each on Johannesburg, any aspect, any style.

When we met to compare our stories, deciding to repeat the entertaining exercise, we discussed all sorts of other things, including an international conference of sixty thousand-odd delegates due to be held in Jo'burg five months hence.

A few days later we joined up the dots: Johannesburg, loads of foreigners descending on the city, short stories, different writing. Let's ask local and foreign journalists to write a thousand words on Jozi, any aspect, any style. We'll set a tight deadline in order to have the book on sale in time for the influx of conference delegates. And we'll donate the royalties to children affected by Aids.

The idea took off instantly. Writers seized it with such enthusiasm that we were soon buried in contributions, agonising over selection. We sped on with hardly a hitch, presenting the manuscript to Penguin South Africa within seven weeks of our decision to compile the book.

Adam and I had fun editing *From Jo'burg to Jozi*. Coming from different backgrounds and perspectives, we encountered a few issues along the way. One was the South African writers' use of the term 'blacks', which foreigners sometimes find brash or demeaning (though they seldom complain about 'whites' in the same way) even when hearing all South Africans, from the President down, using these unambiguous terms.

So, here it is: *From Jo'burg to Jozi*. From concept to book-shelf in five months. That's Johannesburg energy for you!

Heidi Holland
June 2002

From Jo'burg to Jozi

Johannesburg is an infamous city. Many outsiders know it as little more than an arena for violence, crime and shocking inequality. It certainly has very serious problems, but insiders, those who live and work in the city, have another view of southern Africa's biggest metropolis. For them Jo'burg is not a forbidding place of walls, malls, casinos and shacks, but a city with history, rich networks of people, bizarre and attractive architecture, a lively economic pulse. It is an edgy, energetic city, which draws new arrivals from across the continent. In this book sixty journalists and writers have each offered a short story, a poem, an anecdote or a piece of reportage that reflects a view of the infamous city. Some, inevitably, worry about grime and crime, fading glory and general decay. Others have looked for a side of Johannesburg that is less well known to the world. This book offers readers a broad view of a city so badly maligned.

Johannesburg, like any city in the world, has many faces. But when I first decided to move here, I was given warnings it is a rotten and threatening place that you should flee, not enter. Some fellow journalists from London suggested that I should move my office to Cape Town, or at least to sleepy Pretoria. They said there is such crime, such violence, high walls, electric fences, the city has imprisoned itself and has ceased to be a civilised place. South Africans in London and even in Cape Town seemed to think that it was as foolish to move to Jo'burg as to set up home in Grozny, Kabul or Bogota.

They were wrong of course, but such advice was chilling. My guidebooks were no better and none had a good word for the city. The author of one very respectable guidebook, which was published at the turn of the millennium, thinks the city of gold is terribly tarnished. The best thing to do with Johannesburg, he says, is to avoid it. His hottest tip for where to sleep when visiting Jo'burg, is Bloemfontein, a sleepy backwater 400 kilometres away. He goes on:

> '. . . the name Johannesburg is synonymous with crime and violence – a crazy mix of Blade Runner and Escape from New York – and a visit here almost carries a government health warning. Those brave, foolish or single-minded souls who actually spend some time in Jo'burg will experience an essential side of post apartheid South Africa, and be rewarded with their very own tales of danger, excitement and mugging . . .'

That a guidebook was so gloomy worried me, since in my earlier travels to countries enduring war, a repressive government or chronic crime, the guides have always been quite cheery. Sure, there are problems, they would normally suggest, but take care and you'll be fine. The odds are generally with you and if most locals survive, well, then why won't you? Backpacking in Peru, sneaking in to report from Burma, or poking around in Sierra Leone, the cautiously optimistic books have always proved right. South Africa is not at war and has a rather friendly government, but Johannesburg apparently does not deserve the stoical, hopeful approach. The books

2

suggested that Jo'burg is so threatening it ranks in a separate, hopeless category all of its own.

Visitors here will hopefully realise that such gloom is unwarranted. But it fits a pessimistic trend towards Africa, as outsiders take ever more sceptical views of the continent. Any reader looking for a book on Johannesburg would be hard-pressed to find a kind word written about the city. More serious South African writers, the Coetzees, Gordimers, Brinks, have such vinegary, worried views 'you won't want to go to South Africa at all' warned a friend. 'Their murders, rapes, moral decay and despair would be no advert for your new home.'

Readers might turn instead to explorer-writers, journalists and adventurers, who traipse through danger and revel in it later on. Many travellers write about today's Africa, and have braved the continent's richest city, but none gives a friendly account of the place. One man who recently pottered from Zanzibar to Cape Town saved his harshest words for this metropolis. It has a 'post-apocalyptic air' he wrote; much of the city has been abandoned and the streets crawl with 'gangsters and *tsotsis*'. 'Everyone had personal knowledge of someone who had died violently.' Another writer, an African-American who reported from Africa for several years and even put up with living in Nairobi, Kenya, said that in the late 1990s doctors in Jo'burg's northern suburbs were 'prescribing more antidepressants than ever before', while illegal drug use was also shooting up. He described Jo'burg as a volatile, comical and bizarre mix of the rich world and the poor one, a city of casinos, shopping malls and swimming pools put cheek to cheek with a poor, undeveloped, resentful mass. That sounded like much of America to me. Others wrote that Jo'burg is more like a frontier town, a part of the wild west, and it remains a harsh mining city of roughnecks and the lawless.

Of course they are not inventing the problems in the city.

Understandably writers are shocked to pick up one of the big local newspapers – the *Sowetan* or *The Star* – at breakfast, to be greeted over their toast with tales of murder and front page pictures of corpses. Almost as disturbing are little signs of disorder and collapse. The way Jo'burgers drive, with scant thought for speed limits, road rules, insurance and sobriety is disconcerting if you come from a more law-abiding place. A measure of anarchy, said one friend after a visit here, is that even the most conformist learn to defy the rules: he recalled a drive one night with Germany's ambassador to South Africa, a man one might expect to be a model of respectful caution, who had furiously plunged through red light after red light, giving more thought to carjackers than to the law of the land or oncoming cars.

But these writers have neglected another side to Johannesburg, the cultural and cosmopolitan buzz, the mixture of Africa and the west, the youthful energy and edge. They ignore that something, perhaps the lure of money, excitement, work, bright lights and opportunity, something continues to draw thousands of newcomers to the city every day. These people see hope in the city, not despair. They also have a different name for Jo'burg, one that sheds all connection with the old, white mining city and instead promotes its youthful, African, edgy reputation. They call the city Jozi.

This book is not an effort to rehabilitate Johannesburg. That will only happen when the city's real problems of unemployment, crime and especially violence begin to abate. There are some reasons to be hopeful, as a few unofficial statistics suggest violent crime is dropping sharply and as anyone with open eyes can see, redevelopment is beginning downtown. There is also anecdotal evidence that Johannesburg, Jozi, could be on the road to recovery: architects say they are very busy in the town centre building residential property; small traders report good business from downtown; the council has a thirty-year plan to reclaim the whole city; police say that their stronger presence is having an effect even in notorious Hill-brow; private security companies say closed circuit television cameras have slashed crime in the centre of town. That is all good news, though it is probably too early to celebrate.

Instead, this book is intended to be an enjoyable read, which might also broaden readers' understanding of the city and modify its notorious name. Johannesburg has a reputation, which is no mean success for an African city. Ask an average European what he thinks of Kampala or Kigali and he will not be sure if you are talking about towns or types of disease. An American might be equally bamboozled by Douala, Tana or Dar es Salaam, plausibly goods found in an exotic delicatessen. Many non-Africans, imagining villages and jungle, might even be surprised to learn that this continent is scattered with sizeable towns and cities. But most know something of Jo'burg.

I know from my own early prejudice against the place that many outsiders think little of Johannesburg. When I drove for the first time from the international airport, and Africa's most striking urban skyline loomed up under a dazzling winter sun, that reputation nagged at my nerves. I wondered why on earth was I moving to a world hotspot for murders and violence. I was told that so many criminals are produced here that one minister had suggested making the city's mineshafts into dungeons. Aids is so common and deadly, I had read, that many urban graveyards are now completely full. Guns are so prevalent, unemployment so high and the legacy of violent, racist repression so strong that many thousands of people were fleeing each year.

That night I got lost for the first time, driving panicked through the city's deserted, featureless, northern suburbs, expecting a hijack, a robbery or worse if I drifted towards Hillbrow or downtown. I barely dared stop to consult a map, and when eventually I stumbled on my guesthouse in Melville it was with a deep surge of relief and gratitude for the secure metal fences and the sharp click of the key. Only later I realised how safe that night's journey had actually been. Terrible expectations, the reputation, of the city had helped to create my fear.

Since then I have found Johannesburg a diverse, lively and enjoyable city to live in, despite its problems and its doomsayers. And I have gradually understood that the view from guidebooks, the sour South African expats, and sometimes from Jo'burg residents themselves, is restrictively narrow. So many white middle-aged Jo'burgers have introduced themselves by suggesting I should flee, that I wonder if we see the same place at all. I have been told that some white residents in comfortable and quiet suburbs will not leave their houses after dark, let alone venture downtown. Jo'burg is clearly unloved by strangers, and by some of its own.

Given time Johannesburg's reputation will change, perhaps after it becomes really African and is more generally known as Jozi. One hopeful sign that the city is ready to move on is its willingness to face an uncomfortable recent history. Visitors and residents alike should make their way to the city's newest, and best, cultural attraction, the Apartheid Museum. It is dedicated to telling the whole story of a wicked, racist regime that affected all South Africans. Here a strong theme emerges from Johannesburg and its huge satellite townships, notably Soweto. It tells how racist prejudice developed into a modern, industrial system of exploitation as the gold mines of Johannesburg demanded huge supplies of cheap (black)

labour. Even so, the city remained relatively mixed, in racial terms, until national leaders took up the perverse ideology of apartheid and forced the segregation and removal of whole communities. A renowned example was the destruction of the mostly black and bohemian quarter Sophiatown, which was replaced with an all-white suburb called, astoundingly, Triomf.

But it was also here that racial repression and then apartheid were attacked from within: more than a century ago Mahatma Gandhi, who worked as a barrister in nearby Pretoria, preached tolerance in Johannesburg; later African National Congress leaders delivered powerful, humane speeches at their trials in the city's courts; Nelson Mandela recently recalled how, during his treason trial and later in prison, he would be jeered and told he should have stayed home in rural Transkei. 'But for me, I told them, Johannesburg is now my home. I would go back to Johannesburg.' For many other men and women who would become ANC leaders and anti-apartheid campaigners – I have particularly strong memories of Archbishop Desmond Tutu and Winnie Mandela from news reports in the 1980s – Johannesburg also became home.

The city's own people did much to undermine apartheid: early bus boycotts by residents of Alexandra township showed a street-based political movement could grow; then student protests in Soweto in the 1970s showed how strong it had become. Balancing violence on the streets was the emergence of an educated black business class and of union leaders, like Cyril Ramaphosa, who would help guide a peaceful transition. Even some of Johannesburg's white businessmen realised by the late 1970s that political change would have to come, and they began to make early contact with black partners.

Seen from this other standpoint, Johannesburg is a prouder, more hopeful place, which deserves credit for helping to put an end to a morally corrupt regime. While it is true that much racial prejudice remains – even pet dogs in the white suburbs bark most fiercely at people with black skins – at least it is no longer the ideology of the state. Where many people were once humiliated and barred from living, eating or entering certain areas, the city is now a free, lively, multicultural and relatively mixed hub. Where police could routinely harass and intimidate the majority of the city's residents, people can now move about without fear of arbitrary arrest and torture. Of course terrible divisions remain and new problems have come about. But these are more normal, the sort suffered in other parts of the world: there is crime and inequality, and a de facto segregation between the rich in leafy suburbs and the poor in townships; but some of that is common to almost every city, and at least it is no longer a strict division by race or by law.

One place that made this clear to me is a community of artists in Newtown who have studios in a disused bag factory near the Market Theatre (where anti-apartheid plays were famously performed in a converted fruit market). Among the visiting and resident painters and sculptors is a group of established local artists. A favourite subject of one of them is street life, skylines and buildings of Johannesburg at night. He explained that a curfew once forced black South Africans out of the city each evening, banishing them to townships like Alexandra, also known as the Dark City because of its lack of electricity. Now Jo'burg's lights and the nightlife are there for all. For some of the contributors to this book, as for the artists, trips to Johannesburg and its lights are remembered with a thrill, because the city at night was for so long out of bounds.

When Johannesburg recovers, it is likely to surge to success. Just as New York, Cape Town and other cities have been able to clean up their centres and encourage businesses and residents to move back to once crime-ridden places, Johannesburg will do the same. An official council plan to recover the city and bring it to world standards by 2030 aims to make Jozi like 'a London or San Francisco'. That may be a long time to wait, but most exciting in the short term is news that more people are choosing to move back into downtown Johannesburg than are fleeing it. Young, professional South Africans are daring to live close to their jobs, rather than commute for hours each day. Perhaps the tide has turned.

As Jozi grows it will leave its all-white mentality long behind and South Africans should see a city that succeeds by shedding its European, twentieth-century ambitions by becoming a part of Africa and a global city combined. Jozi aspires to global standards, but it needs also to be part of its continent and to lead Africa just as New York leads America, or Hong Kong leads much of Asia. These cities are cosmopolitan, dynamic, and mix local cultures with imported ones. In the same way Johannesburg should grow into Jozi, happily tied to the rest of Africa, welcoming skilled and useful immigrants from north of the Limpopo river as much as it attracts businessmen and ideas from the rest of the world.

Already Jozi, the continent's big apple, should lay claim to be the capital city of Africa, if such an idea makes sense. True, Lagos has more people, but the general area around Jozi, with eight million people, is richer. Africa's Manhattan is a square mile or so of a city suburb, Sandton. Nairobi or Kinshasa are more central in Africa, but greater Johannesburg is the heart of the continent's economy, employing one in eight of all South Africans with formal jobs. Oil money aside, the largest chunk of foreign investment in Africa comes through South Africa and its businesses, most of them in and around Johannesburg.

South Africa is an economic giant compared with its African fellows. Gauteng province which includes Jo'burg and Pretoria has wealth, an economy and drive that would be envied by most African countries. A fifth of South Africa's exports are produced in Jo'burg, and twice that amount passes out of the country through the city. Three out of every four South African big businesses have their head offices here. Mining houses, banks, insurance companies, some of the biggest universities in Africa and the largest contingent of Africa's foreign press corps (and probably the largest, most professional domestic one too) are here as well.

In Africa, all roads lead to Jozi. Follow planes in Africa's skies – from London, Atlanta, Delhi – or trace the dust behind Africa's buses or the direction of footprints, and you are more likely to end up in Jo'burg than anywhere else. One Ethiopian friend described how he had made his way south, through Kenya and down the continent, always heading for the hope of a new life in Johannesburg. A British businessman, stuck in poverty-stricken Madagascar, recently reminisced about the bright lights of South Africa's faraway big town and summed it up well: 'Ah Johannesburg, the world's most underrated city.'

What is there in comparison? In what other city do sparks fly from your fingertips in austral winter and dramatic lightning storms welcome the end of most summer afternoons? And if nature's static doesn't excite you, there is usually something human to keep your hair on end. So many of Africa's nominal capitals are sleepy little towns, barely connected to their own countries. Cities like Freetown, Maputo, Dar es Salaam, Luanda and Cape Town are charming coastal accessories, but they barely cling to the continent by their fingertips. Those colonial towns, at the mouths of rivers, around harbours, strung along beaches, turn their backs on Africa, on their 'up-country' cousins. But Johannesburg is itself upcountry, it is also a mile or so up in the air, and like any great city it beckons the world.

Though without embassies or a presidential palace, great spokes of roads arrive from all directions, train tracks snake here and thousands of taxi buses whizz to the centre. Crest a hill as you drive south from Pretoria, or stare from one of the city's large parks, and Jo'burg's towers rise as proudly as Oz above the poppy fields. People follow those tracks and pour to Jozi from all over the continent. Well-educated Zimbabweans thrive in the city, joining generations of Mozambican miners, Nigerian traders of various sorts, waiters from Congo, Ethiopian fortune-seekers, British expatriates, East Europeans and the rest. When South Africa learns to benefit from its migrants, just as America and Australia draw enormous economic strength from new arrivals, it will make sense also to talk, as the national airline does, of living a South African dream.

Jozi is young and will transform. At little more than a century, it lacks the pedigree of Istanbul, Baghdad or Jerusalem, but there are signs that humans have lived here for thousands of years. They will remain a long time yet. Though the city is blighted with a bad name, there is also a deep sympathy for it. Residents are fond of telling stories, urban myths, about their home. A popular one is that Jo'burg has more trees than any other city, which were planted by miners who were paid a penny per sapling in order to grow timber for mine props. Look over the forested northern suburbs and the myth might just be true.

Three of us had the idea for this book. It grew partly from the passion Jo'burgers have for talking about their city, but it began with a late-night discussion between Heidi Holland, Anne Hammerstad and myself. We realised that journalists and writers have strong opinions about Jozi – opinions that go beyond stories of crime and violence which so easily find space in our newspapers. We also discussed how few books there are about Johannesburg, and how those that do exist are mostly dusty tomes on the early gold miners. Heidi Holland and I decided to approach a broad range of local, foreign, old and young writers, from as many different backgrounds as possible, to ask each for one thousand words on the city. We found a pent-up wish to describe how Johannesburg is richer, more varied and more stimulating than its terrible reputation suggests.

The range of contributions might help deepen readers' appreciation of Jozi, though there has been no attempt to polish up the city or censor its grimier, nastier side. The choice of subject and of style was each writer's own. Each writer was free to express any opinion. Unsurprisingly for journalists, many of the pieces that follow are factual, argumentative reportage. But there are also contributions of fiction, anecdotes, emails, reminiscences, poetry and direct observation.

How were the writers chosen? Broadly this is a book by journalists and writers who have lived for some time in Johannesburg. Most have English as their mother tongue, but not all. Some of the writers are well known and well established, some are early in their careers. South African readers looking through the contents pages will find some familiar authors: Rian Malan makes a case for loving Jo'burg; Anthony Sampson recalls Sophiatown of half a century ago; John Matshikiza recounts his return to Soweto after years of exile.

Readers will also find many journalists who write as correspondents for well-known newspapers: among others, Christopher Munnion of Britain's *Daily Telegraph* tells of reporting on Johannesburg from a downtown pub and his successor Tim Butcher relates the history of a single tree; several writers for South Africa's *Mail & Guardian* are present here along with the *Sunday Times* and *Sunday Sun;* also here are the Africa editor of the *Financial Times* and correspondents for America's *Newsday* and *Baltimore Sun,* Norway's *Dagbladet,* Britain's *Independent*, the Reuters news service and my own paper, *The Economist*.

The broadcast media is here too. Barnaby Phillips of the BBC compares life in Lagos, Nigeria, with his new home; Jonah Hull of AP Television News remembers the 1994 elections and makes a stinging and unsettling challenge to the hidden beliefs and values of white South Africans today. Some characters of Johannesburg life are also present: Doc Bikitsha, a veteran black journalist, has drawn on decades of memories to present his own Johannesburg; Arthur Maimane remembers Jozi's recent history and how important it is to be streetwise; Zakes Mda reflects on how outsiders are treated in Johannesburg; Hilda and Rusty Bernstein, who both played prominent roles in the city's history, each contribute here too.

There are also laments in this book. Derrick Thema is saddened by the city's lost sparkle and pride; Heidi Holland and Mungo Soggot each remind readers how prevalent and worrying crime remains; Jann Turner tells a moving story of her employee's battle against an assault and then against HIV; Stephen Gray's description of a failing institution may be taken by some as a metaphor for the city.

At times the strictest definition of journalist was pushed aside so we could bring in original short stories or extracts from novelists and other writers: Veronique Tadjo of Côte d'Ivoire makes an evocative appeal to the city to wake up; Phaswane Mpe, a young South African novelist, writes on Hillbrow; Christopher Hope says he wants to hear the heart of Jo'burg beating again; Ivan Vladislavić concludes the book with a slightly longer story on the changing city and his response as a writer.

It is impossible to mention each short story or poem here, but readers will dip in as they choose, finding modern Johannesburg's gyms, malls, casinos, sports stadiums, townships, herbal markets and restless nights pushed up against an old Chinese community, memories of the treason trials and evidence of ancient man. And each reader will take out something different. What strikes me is how many writers, despite its reputation, are inspired or hopeful about this infamous city.

Adam Roberts
Johannesburg, Jozi
June 2002

Thoughts on Johannesburg's Centenary

(while by the Jukskei River at Broederstroom)

Lionel Abrahams

There is no city as old as a river,
as old as this minor stream
whose millennia have sculpted the veld.
The wiser cities lie down with great rivers
to learn what rivers teach of time,
or with the timelessness of seas;
but my city's mazed metal of hurried streets
has buried the small white waters.

What if my wandering clan had given me
one of those old wise cities to be born in?
I would have claimed that borrowed ancestry
of mellow stones and streets, embraced

the longings and learning of that home,
spelled my name in its memorial marks.
Instead they gave me to the raw spawn of payable lode,
attracting loose acquisitive pioneers,
the hungry and threatened, chancers and transients
– swelling by gross promises and harsh divisions
over unhistoric farms and hills.

Born but never Native here (of Europe-stranger kin,
that skin), I've known no other place to claim.
Heir to the Book, I find and lose my living myths
more in these too changeable streets.
I learned to spread from hollow roots
patches of familiar turf:
time gave my stories to some names and contours;
certain settings of my years, my selves, won my affection,
enrolled me in a Masonry of esoteric love.
I belong with the unbelonging, and this world
of second generation strangers, all its cheap renewal,
gives me my only earthed tradition,
all prospect of a self-built meaning I can claim.

How can you love what changes too swiftly,
too swiftly changes and changes again?
A river is momently different, and daily,
but the slow living banks hold the shape of memory –
the self can stay while the river runs
and we can love the river.
But Jo'burg's straight streets hardly
survive their shouting rivers of traffic;
this place owes too little to time,
too much to appetite and rage
and guilty self-contempt –
it eats and tears itself . . . renews . . . renews . . .

A man stays naked at the dumb mouth of the cave,
shivering like a dog beneath thunder –
a man and his streets are disposable trash
if the town does not bequeath to his passing eye
old shapes told about in tales,
histories held visible in shapes
that he knows will still be seen beyond his time.

If all who must leave
take their insights and go,
take the innocence they fear to lose
and go,
and the rage burns out,
and the gold gives out,
yet the Name of the city endures –
magnet and conduit for memory's gathering –
this place may draw together, discover
the richer reasons of its century,
may hear the singing of its hundred-year-old course.

Lionel Abrahams was born in Johannesburg in 1928. He was the publisher-editor of a Johannesburg literary magazine and of several books, and is a creative writing teacher and critic. He is also the author of four volumes of poetry, two of fiction, and a miscellany. This poem won the Olive Schreiner Prize for Poetry in 1986.

Kum Saan

Darryl Accone

The gravestone cast a long shadow, even at this early hour of the day. Ah Nang began to feel dizzy as he looked at the thicket of compacted vertical, horizontal and diagonal characters chiselled into its granite face. A wisp of incense caught at his nose, insistent in its acrid sweetness.

'Father, whose grave is this? It is not anyone from our family. Why are we here? What are we doing at this grave?'

'The man buried here,' said Ah Nang's father, 'did a very sad thing, hurting the community, and then a very brave thing to win his honour back. And that made them all ashamed for not sticking by him, despite what he did, because he was one of us – and what he first did, he did with good intentions.'

'What did he do? Why is his grave so far from the others? Why is it facing the other way, with its back to the morning sun?'

'Come, we'll tell you on the way home,' said the boy's

mother, brushing red dust and dead grass from her skirt before joining her hands and inclining them three times towards the tombstone.

When they had left, the freshly tended grave kept its eternal vigil, looking in vain for the rays of the sun to stroke its head and caress the name and inscriptions scored into its grey stone.

CHOW KWAI FOR
1885 – 1907

Gave his life for the community that abandoned him

Rest in peace and honour

From the Chinese of Johannesburg, grieving that they drove a countryman to pass so early from this world

As they strolled towards the main gate of the cemetery, mother and father explained, as simply as they could, about Chow Kwai For. This is the story they told.

Many years ago, things in this country were not as they are now. People were strictly divided by colour. The whites were in charge and they kept for themselves the best of everything: jobs, houses, clothes, services, food. Everyone who was 'non-white' was seen as inferior. Although the 'non-whites' were by far and away more numerous than the whites, they were the servants and labourers, the second- and third-class citizens with no chance of advancement and no say in how the country was run.

One day, the government said that the Chinese, too, would have to carry pass books – identity documents that 'non-whites', but not whites, had to keep on themselves at all times. The Chinese refused.

The Chinese consul-general and local community leaders spoke out against the pass book. The community stood fast against the government. There were street protests and the famous lawyer Mohandas Gandhi stood in solidarity with the Chinese.

But Chow Kwai For had just arrived from China; actually, from Heinan Island, south of the mainland. He was hoping to work in Kum Saan, the gold mountain of Johannesburg, in the land of Nam Fee Chow, this South Africa of ours. He did not want to cause trouble. He believed one should obey the law, even more so in a foreign country. So Chow Kwai For went to the home affairs office and got his pass book. He had his fingerprints taken and put in the book, as well as into the central records. He left the government offices smiling, sure that his stay would be trouble-free because he had followed the rules.

Somehow, perhaps because he spoke a different dialect of Chinese, he had not known of the community's position. When he found out, he was embarrassed but gave it not much thought: he could not break the law. He wanted to fit in to this new country, this very different society.

But just as they say that blood is thicker than water – that family are closer than friends – so it is with nationality. The Chinese felt betrayed by Chow Kwai For. They thought he had valued fitting in to this uneven society, where Chinese had few rights and no respect, above remaining faithful to his community.

Also, because one Chinese had a pass book, it could have meant all Chinese would have to. So angry were the Chinese that they did not have anything to do with the unfortunate young man. No one would speak to him. They refused to sell him goods, food, clothing, herbal medicines. There was no place in Chinatown that would accept him as a lodger.

In hope, Chow Kwai For carried on, believing that at some time he would be forgiven. But even though the government could not force the pass book on the community, Chow Kwai For's crime was not forgotten. He was not forgiven. An outcast, he struggled on for a few years but the loneliness, the hatred and the shame in the eyes of the community were too much for him.

One day, in his dingy room in a corrugated iron shack, he hanged himself. He left behind a note saying that he hoped his death would cancel the community's dishonour and that his family name would no longer be held in disgrace.

Still, Chow Kwai For was buried far from other Chinese, because he was regarded as bad luck. Vengeful elders said that the grave should face westwards, like those of murderers who did not deserve ever to see the rising sun. Chow Kwai For, they said, was as bad as a killer because of the way he had put the community in danger. That is why the grave is so far from the other Chinese.

But then, because community and country are closer than adopted home, the Chinese felt very guilty at how they had driven one of their own sons to leave the world so soon. After a while, the community understood that the shame, dishonour and disgrace was theirs. So they put up a tombstone to honour the young man who had wanted just to fit in. And they remembered that fitting in is what all people who come to new and strange lands want to do, in some or other way.

Darryl Accone has worked with words for over twenty years, as a reporter, critic, columnist and editor. He exchanged hometown Pretoria for the city lights of Jo'burg in the late 1970s. Life since has been a coup de ville: Yeoville, Troyeville, Pleasantville (a northern suburbs townhouse while suffering temporary loss of reason) and Melville. He is researching and writing the story of his Chinese-South African family.

As old as history itself

Sue Armstrong

I love Johannesburg. Every time my plane comes in to land, circling over the scruffy yellow mine dumps, the thin, thrusting skyscrapers and glinting glass of central Johannesburg, the snaking motorways encircling the city, the turquoise spangles of swimming pools and psychedelic splashes of bougainvillaea in suburban gardens, the serried ranks of new township developments mushrooming out to the open veld, and the rashes of untidy squatter settlements, my chest tightens with excitement. Jo'burg is in your face, and overfamiliar from the moment you touch down.

This city isn't encumbered by pageantry, steeped in tradition, or smothered by history – though its history, unbeknownst to most visitors or even residents, is as old as history itself. Johannesburg sits in the midst of one of the richest palaeontological sites in the world – a honeycomb of dolomite caves full of the fossil remains of our human ancestors from several million years ago. There's Sterkfontein, a deep gash in the bleak, grassy hills of the highveld that was originally opened up as a lime quarry, but is ranked today as one of the richest hominid fossil sites in the world. In seventy years of exploration it has yielded hundreds of specimens of apemen, as well as fossils of our first truly human ancestor, *Homo habilis*, along with a mass of the stone tools that gave *habilis* his name. Sterkfontein was the last resting place, some three and a half million years ago, of a person now known as Little Foot, who leapt to international fame in 1995 when four of his bones were discovered in a forgotten box of unsorted rubble from the caves. They showed that early man was likely to have been a chimpanzee-like tree-climber rather than just a wanderer of the plains.

Across the valley from Sterkfontein is Swartkrans, another dusty digging and a classic site that has turned up masses of key pieces of the human jigsaw. In 1986 the small team of excavators who labour with painstaking precision in that lonely spot uncovered layer upon layer of burnt bone left in the caves one to one and a half million years ago. It was the earliest evidence then of the controlled use of fire – pre-dating by perhaps one million years the previous record from Zhoukoudian, China, of fire associated with Peking Man about 400 000 years ago. Some palaeontologists believe it was this new tool, fire, rather than language or use of weapons that finally gave us the edge over the apemen, and power to dominate the natural world. Whatever the truth, the discovery out there on the highveld was hugely significant, for practically everything in our modern world is the product of fire technology.

Not many miles from Swartkrans and Sterkfontein is Gladysvale, a cave system set in a beautiful stretch of hills studded with thorn trees and shaggy aloes. Here, in 1992, the complete skeleton of a creature unlike anything ever seen before was unearthed after someone had spotted a rib cage sticking out of the cave wall. Something like a cross between a dog and a bear and believed to have lived about two and a half million years ago, the creature was curled in a foetal position in what must have been its lair, since fossilised faeces were scattered around. Its stomach contained fossilised bits of mice and birds and the seeds of a tropical palm. The perfectly preserved 'bear-dog', as it was nicknamed, was a fantastic find – most such creatures died violently or were eaten quickly and their bones scattered. The theory is that it was caught in a mudslide as it slept.

But that's the great beauty of cave sites compared with the lake beds and river sediments in which most fossils are found – creatures have turned to stone near where they lived, rather than being scattered and smashed by the elements. Our ancestors probably sheltered in those caves around Johannesburg, or were dragged there by creatures that hunted and killed them on the plains. You can often recreate the environment they lived in, a moment in time, and even sometimes the instant of death, from bits of evidence found nearby – other fossilised plants and animals and even grains of pollen. These recreations are sometimes rather fanciful: a palaeontologist isn't above telling you a creature walked upright, swung from the trees, or lived in small family groups from the evidence of a single tooth. But then the essential qualities for making your name in palaeontology are 'the patience of Job and a bloody good imagination!' I was told in Johannesburg by Phillip Tobias, one of South Africa's most eminent practitioners.

The imagination is infectious. Once you have handled the awesome, ancient bones of our ancestors stored in the anatomy department of Johannesburg's medical school, or scrambled – sometimes on hands and knees – through the dank, dark tunnels of Jo'burg caves, you fancy you can feel some primordial pulse below the glitzy surface of the modern city. And when one of the magnificent highveld thunderstorms rages overhead in all its elemental splendour, you are reminded that these are the elements that fashioned us – here, in this place – millions of years ago.

Sue Armstrong is a freelance writer and broadcaster who worked for *New Scientist* magazine and BBC World Service radio from southern Africa in the 1980s and 1990s. She has written extensively about the spread of Aids for the World Health Organisation.

Watch my lips

Len Ashton

Bennie Snyman smiled like a trapped rat. A mirthless reflex, suggestive of dodgy dentistry and inscrutable divine dispensation. It was unfair. For Bennie was seriously disadvantaged by his grin. Snarling when you meant to convey amiability was a hard thing to bear.

There were those few who recognised the questing loneliness beneath the blue pinstripe suit, but most people patronised Bennie. Even when the neighbours told his Mom and Dad, my, hasn't he done well. Massive Pa Snyman regularly made it clear that he would have preferred a beefy son to sustain the illusion that the family might leave Jo'burg one day to farm mealies again in some dusty paradise. Somewhere near Bethal, maybe. But what chance was there of that consummation when the one and only offspring turned out to be a runt? Just like his mother. Maybe Pa would have been able to hold on to the farm if his wife and son had had more meat on them.

Still, Bennie was a lawyer. Qualified. That was something, and the neighbours knew it. Last year he was a legal clerk, hardly able to afford lunch. Now he was on his way, blue suit and all. It hadn't been easy. The other boys had given him a hard time at school, and all that swotting hadn't persuaded the street that Bennie was a real man, like the kids who broke things and stole things and hit each other. Despite the odds, he was becoming a criminal lawyer. Criminal, naturally, because petty thievery was the secret undertow of the neighbourhood.

Six months later, it happened.

Bennie fell in love. Not with some nice, clean girl who could type. No, not Bennie. He fell for a gang. A whole gang of brawling ruffians who came to him for advice when they were questioned by the constabulary in the matter of a missing Toyota. The leading lights were the brothers Botha, a trio of intellectually challenged but entertainingly vigorous youths who were concerned to obtain the means to seduce girls. Bennie had admired their antics at a distance during adolescence, and the brothers had condescended occasionally to cuff him in abstracted acknowledgement of his existence.

Now they sought his wisdom. It was an intoxicating situation. Not only did the Bothas share their fears of the law with him but, in their unselfconscious way, admitted him to their secret councils regarding fantastical get-rich-quick schemes, sex and rugby. Bennie, in his new elder statesman role, affected avuncular amusement at the boys' bizarre notions, but tried sincerely to lead them in the paths of righteousness. After all, they lived in the same street (pending the rising young lawyer's elevation to a bachelor flat in opulent Cyrildene), so it was right and proper that Bennie should be seen to show an interest in the well-being of his less conventional neighbours.

Bennie's employers were not aware that he was spending

a good deal of after-hours time with the Bothas. They would have disapproved. The boys had been in trouble before and were known to be less than punctilious about payment of legal fees.

When the Toyota affair dragged on expensively – because certain state witnesses abruptly and mysteriously proved reluctant to incriminate members of the gang – Bennie warned the lads that Smithers, Blomkamp and Partners would be demanding a little cash encouragement in the near future if they were to persist in their efforts to prove the boys' innocence.

The boys heard him without comment, gazed at each other thoughtfully, and then disappeared for two days. On their return, they pressed a substantial sum of cash on Bennie and asked whether they might store certain goods at his house. Now Bennie wasn't stupid – the law degree gained in difficult circumstances proved that – but he was vulnerable. Disarmed by their trust, he agreed to store the parcels. Foolish Bennie.

When the gang appeared in court at an interim hearing, the young lawyer and his clients were seen to be a mite too familiar with each other than was deemed proper for an officer of the law. But Bennie was flattered by the Bothas' attention and failed to observe the disapproval.

Significantly, Bennie no longer flashed his old death's head grin when under pressure. The boys' respect had given him confidence and a new personal dignity. The face he now presented to the world was one of restraint rather than fear.

But the boys were incapable of restraint. One day they tumbled into Bennie's home and delved furtively into their parcels while their mentor gazed at the ceiling or pretended to riffle through the case papers. Then, the following evening, the Bothas pulled up in raucous triumph aboard a flamboyant old Cadillac, with girls to match. That brought the neighbours out in a susurration of admiration.

'Come on, Bennie,' they yelled. 'Come for a ride.'

And Bennie went.

Everybody saw him being welcomed and admitted to the uproarious camaraderie. Everybody saw them cruising in that absurd old Caddy. Next day, the cops arrived to search Bennie's house. They removed the parcels from under the kitchen sink and asked awkward questions. Bennie was unable to answer the interrogation satisfactorily and the ordeal triggered his old, abject, propitiatory rat grin. But, when he appeared afterwards in the dock in company with the boys, he was calm and unsmiling. Even when Mr Snyman senior stumped into the courtroom and proclaimed to all and sundry that there was no chance now of his getting back to the land. Mrs Snyman, of course, said nothing. She never had and never would.

They say the boys look after Bennie in jail. He helps them with letters and bureaucracy. His father sold the blue suit to a man who said he was searching for God and had only thirty rand. At Christmastime Mr Snyman sent Bennie a body-building book, second hand from the charity stall. His mother sent a postcard of Jesus simpering below a halo edged surprisingly with roses and daffodils.

Len Ashton has been a journalist since the fourteenth century, or thereabouts, in South Africa and London. He lives in Cape Town and is now working freelance for newspapers and magazines.

Kwame doesn't worry

Ruth Ansah Ayisi

As I tried in vain to dodge one of the ever-deepening potholes near our home in Mozambique's capital Maputo, my eight-year-old son Kwame sighed. 'Mum, I wish Mozambique had never had a war. Then it would have had nice roads like those in Johannesburg.'

We had just returned from Johannesburg. Kwame loved it. He loves the restaurants, especially MacDonald's. He loves the variety of shows and kids' movies. On the rare occasions that kids' movies are shown in Maputo's one good cinema, they are dubbed in Portuguese. 'That's hard work to follow,' says Kwame.

He is also deeply impressed by my friends' large houses with spacious well-kept gardens, with their pet dogs and their blue swimming pools. He accepted, although disappointed, that he was ordered out of a swimming pool in a complex where my friend lived because he 'was not a resident'. It was apparent he was not living there only by his skin colour. My friend is engaged in a constant battle with residents who complain about his guests, most of whom are black Africans.

Nor does Kwame worry about the top security in people's homes. He loves to press the buttons that activate electronic garage gates. Even when a burglar alarm went off on Christmas Eve in my friend's house, and I almost had a heart attack, Kwame was excited, convinced it was Santa Claus with his reindeer. The security company came in full force bearing torches and guns to see if we had an attacker in the grounds. It was reassuring to see the Great Dane, the St Bernard and the friendly, large mongrel dog all wagging their tails, pleased to have attention in the middle of the night. It proved to have been a false alarm. A teenager in the house, thirsty during the night, had forgotten that entering the kitchen would trigger the alarm.

Most of all Kwame loves to shop in Johannesburg's world-beating malls. You can choose between the mock-Italian Montecasino, glitzy Sandton, or the people's mall, Eastgate. It was on one of our shopping expeditions that Kwame saw another side of Johannesburg.

The crowds were friendly and Eastgate seemed a civilised place. Kwame's eyes were everywhere. An elderly woman was carefully threading bright-coloured beads, making the famous Zulu jewellery that is sometimes worn by supermodels. Other traders showed off an array of wooden and iron sculptures – elephants, giraffes of all sizes, impala, you name the creature, it was there in polished splendour.

Kwame manoeuvred me to a toy stall. I steered him clear of the many toy guns, some looking very real. They reminded me that everyone I know in Johannesburg has a story to tell of violent crime either happening to them or to someone close to them.

We compromised. Instead of a gun, he could choose a violent-looking action figure riding a horse. A young black man came up to assist us. He tried to sell us a gun too. But we stuck to the action figure on horseback. He gave us a discount, we paid him one hundred rand and strolled away.

Then an elderly white woman came after us. 'Have you paid for that?' she asked me in a thick Afrikaans accent. I was indignant; she thinks all blacks steal, I thought.

Kwame and I said 'Yes' in unison. She asked more politely, 'Who did you pay?' Kwame looked behind him, spotting the man who had taken our money.

'We paid him,' said Kwame, pointing indelicately.

We were about to walk off when the woman beckoned the man in question. 'Where is the money?' she asked him in a tone suitable for reprimanding a naughty child.

The man replied calmly, 'What money?' He was claiming I had not paid him! I looked around uncertainly for somebody else, thinking it was an embarrassing case of mistaken identity. He was no longer looking friendly.

But Kwame was confident. He stood in front of the man and said: 'We paid YOU.' The man looked Kwame straight in the eye and told him he was 'mad'. Undeterred, Kwame insisted: 'It was him, I'm sure.'

The woman pointed to another man, clearly not the one we had paid. 'Was it that one?'

Kwame sighed as if he was getting bored. 'No, it was him, I know. We paid you,' he insisted, oblivious of the thief's threatening look.

At this, the thief cursed and threw the money at the woman, saying she could take his own money, and he left. She said: 'I have to get rid of him. He's always stealing from us.'

The experience was a dampener on the day. I found myself transformed into a paranoid person in Johannesburg, thinking every young man hanging around was going to rob us. I also kept my eyes out for the thief because I thought he might follow us and 'fix' Kwame.

You can't escape the insecurity, the racial divide, the poverty, I was thinking.

But Kwame had already learned to cope. 'That man is stupid. He tried to rob us,' he declared, looking around for more shopping.

Ruth Ansah Ayisi worked as a journalist in London and Africa for ten years, then for Unicef as an information officer in Mozambique and in New York. She now lives in Maputo, where she works as a communication consultant on HIV/Aids, gender violence and the effects of conflict on children and women.

Servants

Hilda Bernstein

We had working for us a man named Claud, whose wife and children remained in Rhodesia while he worked in Johannesburg.

'If I work in Rhodesia,' he told me once, 'I don't work as hard. A house this size – there would be one boy to do floors, one for garden, one for waiting at table and washing up. But they don't pay you anything.'

Every two or three years Claud returned to his family for about six months. While he was away he would leave a relative or friend in his place to keep his job warm. One year when he wished to go home he brought us a young man who, he said, was his cousin.

Wilson was a handsome, well-built Rhodesian who had never worked in a house before, and who couldn't speak a word of English. Claud showed him what had to be done, and then left for his home.

Wilson was the servant that white South African women dream about. He was quick and quite exceptionally efficient. He knew what had to be done and never had to be told anything, which was just as well because he couldn't understand what I said. In fact he would anticipate the needs of the house and of myself. When he had finished in the house he went outside to work in the garden, and I admired his muscular arms and legs. These were to stand him in good stead.

I felt no one had the right to employ such a man as a domestic servant. His fine physique, his obvious intelligence, his open and pleasant character, showed that he could have made a success of almost any job. Watching Wilson one had the impression that he had the potential to possess great skills. However, I could not help him by telling him he was too good for housework, and giving him the sack. Because Wilson did not have a pass. We knew it, of course, and it was illegal for us to employ him without a pass. But we thought that for the few months Claud was away, he might be able to avoid the police and pickup vans.

He had done what many other Africans from the territories outside South Africa did. He signed a contract to work on the mines as a means to get into South Africa. With all its laws and restrictions, South Africa still offered what the great unskilled masses of southern African countries could not get – opportunities to work at something approaching a reasonable wage. Then, just before his contract expired, he left the mine and made his way to Johannesburg to try to obtain, by one way or another, a pass, a job, and the right to stay.

He had been with us for some time when one day the police came. They were searching for illicit liquor; there was an employee next door who brewed it and sold it to the local domestics. Someone had informed on her, but given the police our house number. They came, searching for liquor, and naturally entered the servant's room and asked Wilson for his pass.

An aggressive policeman arrived at my back door with Wilson in tow and demanded: 'Where's this boy's pass?'

'He hasn't got one,' I replied.

'Don't you know it's illegal to employ a boy without a pass?'

'Yes, I know.'

'Well, you have no right to do it. You could be fined.'

I asked where he would be taken.

'He'll be sent back where he came from.'

'He has all his clothes here,' I said, 'and blankets. And we owe him money for his wages.'

'He'll have a chance to pick them up after they decide what to do with him.'

We spent the whole afternoon and the next morning trying to find out what had happened to Wilson. The local police station denied any knowledge of him; the central station likewise. They arrest thousands for pass offences every week. What do they care about one Wilson without a pass?

Eventually we were told he would be sent to Nigel, a small mining town, where he would be given an opportunity of accepting work on a farm or of returning to Rhodesia. This, like their promise to let him fetch his belongings, was a lie.

A week went by. Then one day when I returned from work a message was waiting for me to phone a Mr van der Westhuizen at a place near Nigel. He had phoned twice.

Without any preliminaries Mr van der Westhuizen said: 'I have your boy Wilson here. He's met with a bit of bad luck and had all his clothes stolen. He's anxious to return to you.'

He told me he was a compound manager on a mine, and that he would lend Wilson some mine clothes and enough for his fare to Johannesburg.

It was winter, and in the evening of a bitterly cold day Wilson arrived at our house, shivering with cold, dressed only in shorts and a singlet, and with a huge weal that extended across his face and down his neck.

With the help of a friend who could speak vernacular, Wilson told us this story.

He was taken to a depot with dozens of other pass offenders. They were loaded on to lorries and driven away into the country.

'But didn't they say you could come back for your clothes?'

'They would not let me come for my clothes.'

They were not brought before any court, nor charged with any crime, nor were any of them given an opportunity of telling relatives or friends that they had been arrested.

'We were taken to a farm,' Wilson said, 'and there they took away everything we were wearing and gave us each a sack.'

This was common practice on many Transvaal farms, where the workers wore an old sack with holes cut for head and arms, as their only clothes, night and day, summer or winter.

On this farm they were locked in a shed every night, let out during the day to work on the lands. The farmer and boss boys assaulted them constantly. That was the whiplash across his face and neck.

'Why did they beat you?'

'For nothing. They say we don't work hard enough. They just beat us.'

After a few days of animal-like work, of beatings, of hard, foul mealie-pap, Wilson decided to run away. There were no toilet facilities in the shed; the African guards armed with kerries would unlock the door to let them out.

'Late one night I went to the guard and told him I must go outside. He said "Put down your sack." I took off my sack and put it on the ground. As he unlocked the door I ran. They ran after me, blowing whistles. I ran fast. It was very dark. After a while I lay down in the ruts in a field, and they ran past me.'

The powerful leg muscles, the coordination that I had

admired in Wilson carried him away from his pursuers. Only someone as young, as strong and as fit could have dared to make such an attempt and succeed.

Now Wilson's story becomes a little odd. He said he lay in the field for a long time; then, stark naked, he ran on through the darkness until he came to the mine, the compound manager of which had phoned me. This man, he said, gave him some food and lent him the clothes and money.

Any compound manager would have known that Wilson was an escaped farm labourer. First, he could not speak any local African language, only Shona. Compound managers know at least one, often more, African languages and would have recognised that he was a Rhodesian. Then for an African to arrive at a mine compound in a farming area, naked and without a pass, saying he had been working in Johannesburg, is highly suspicious. Any normal compound manager would have first checked with local farmers to see if any of their 'boys' were missing.

We think Van der Westhuizen helped escaped farm labourers, and that there must have been talk of him among the workers on the farms.

I still have in my possession the note signed by the compound manager and stamped with the mine stamp that had been Wilson's talisman on his journey back to our home. 'To whom it may concern,' it says. 'Bearer Wilson has been robbed of his clothes, money and documents. He has been assisted to return to his employer in Johannesburg. Kindly permit him to return unhindered.'

What was Van der Westhuizen's motivation? In that small backveld town he was probably a member of the local National Party and a pillar of the Dutch Reformed Church. Probably he too talked contemptuously of 'kaffirs' and yelled at those in his charge. For a man in such a job, in such a town, there would really be no alternative. But the evidence of the note remains, and renews our faith in humanity.

Hilda Bernstein wrote 'Servants' half a century ago. She is a writer, artist, political activist and was a member of Johannesburg's city council in 1943. Her books include *The Rift: The Exile Experience of South Africans* and *The World That Was Ours*.

Tidal Flow

Rusty Bernstein

There are few public occasions of all those apartheid years that I recall with any warmth. One of them came about in June 1957, in downtown Johannesburg. At that time 'down-town' was that small citadel within the city enclosed by railway lines on the north and mine workings on the south, an unsmiling built-up grid of tarmac streets, where only a handful of white adults lived in scattered apartment blocks, with their few domestic retainers out of sight in spartan roof-top quarters. By day it was busy, heads-down, bustling and thrusting, with life adapted to the daily tides, like an island beach. Each morning a tide swept in a flood of suited businessmen and women from *their* homes in the leafy white suburbs, an even larger flood of black workers from *their* hostels or homes in outer 'townships'. Each evening, before the night curfew descended, the tide turned. The human flood flowed out, leaving the downtown buildings beached, the streets quiet and echoing.

That June was a typical apartheid time. The country was in the throes of an attack of paranoia against its perceived 'enemies within' – black liberationists, liberals, radicals and communists. One hundred and fifty-six of the most prominent of them were on trial for their lives on a charge of treason. But on street corners throughout downtown Johannesburg on that day many of the Treason Trial accused and their supporters were taking advantage of a court adjournment and rattling collecting tins under the noses of citizens hurrying to work. Street collections in the city were quite regular, licensed, and strictly controlled by the City Council. But remarkably, this day's collection was in aid of the Treason Trial defence fund itself.

Treason is never a popular cause. Throughout the country, passions for and against the state and its alleged opponents ran high. But downtown, the day's collection passed off peaceably – no police interventions, no brawls, and only a few fierce street-corner arguments. It was as though hostilities and the heavy hand of police repression had been suspended for the day. When the sealed tins were returned to the council officers to be opened and checked, there were over two thousand pounds for the Treason Trial fund – a very considerable sum for those times.

It was an extraordinary, almost bizarre event in a time of political intolerance and repression. It could surely not have happened anywhere except in Johannesburg. Or more precisely, in downtown Johannesburg which was then an exceptional and even contradictory place. The Western Cape is regularly said to have been the then liberal heart of South Africa, because it still held the last tiny remnant of coloured voters on what was otherwise a whites-only voters' roll.

But Johannesburg had a different claim, and a legacy of its own. Within living memory and only sixty years before, it had been no more than a rough mining camp on the bare and inhospitable veld. Johannesburg downtown was still populated by the first and second generation uitlanders who had built Johannesburg out of their dreams of gold or freedom. Deep in their consciousness were the folk memories of times gone by – perhaps of the rough frontier democratism and internationalism of the mining camp; perhaps of life in eastern European lands where radicals and reds had been their only defenders against tsarist and cossack pogroms. Those memories resonated in many downtowners, making Johannesburg a city with a heart; an inner progressive, radical and democratic heart.

Of that, one manifestation was the Treason Trial street collection. Another was the night when hundreds of citizens confronted National Party marchers in the streets, to bar their passage to a celebration of their pro-Nazi 'victory' in the City Hall. There was the survival of the country's most durable public citizens' forum on the City Hall steps, from the time of the great white miners' strikes of 1913 and 1922, until it was finally ended by a combination of fascist thuggery and police persecution. And above all, the fact that throughout the years of apartheid's most draconian repression, downtown donors secretly provided the funding for the survival and growth of the illegal black liberation movements and the Communist Party.

I have returned to Johannesburg from time to time after forty years of absence – as a visitor from abroad. It is my native place, and its history is deep within me. It is a much changed place. Grass has grown over what were then mine dumps of golden sand; suburban streets have been greened with flowering trees and shrubs, but not yet thick enough to black out the forbidding new high boundary walls topped with razor wire, and the proclamations of 'Armed Response'.

Downtown, too, there are changes. The tides have eaten into and eroded much of the character of the old citadel. Many of the great financial and commercial headquarters have flown with the ebb to Sandton and other outer suburbs, leaving only their concrete towers as evidence that they once were there. The money-changers have moved on, and the downtown streets are livelier, more human, and taken over by street traders, noisy, laughing, disputatious.

It feels more human, less driven by greed and ambition. I look to rediscover its radical progressive heart; perhaps it still exists, unseen, in the outer suburbs, but I am no longer aware of it as I once was. Has time corrupted it from within? Or the tides of the new South Africa washed it all away? I remember it not as just an unlovely concrete temple of business, but as the liberal, democratic heart of South Africa. Each time I return I look to see whether it has recovered that heritage. So far in vain.

But I live – and watch – in hope.

Rusty Bernstein, an architect, was born in Johannesburg. He was an accused in the 1956 Treason Trial and the 1964 Rivonia Trial. A former member of the South African Communist Party, his book *Memory Against Forgetting: Memoirs from a Life in South African Politics* was published in 1999.

Romance

Ruth Bhengu

Johannesburg is a city with the power to evoke nostalgia. Whether one is one hundred years old or sweet sixteen, there is always the feeling that something beautiful, something grand has been lost here. It is a feeling that has been passed from generation to generation like a family heirloom.

Every South African has a pet name for Johannesburg. Some call it Egoli, the city of gold, while others know it as Emshishi, Jozi, Kwandonga ziyaduma (where the walls rumble). The elders call it Shishisburg.

There are those who won't set foot in it because they are so scared by the stories of high crime. And there are those who just love it.

Of course the Jo'burg of today with its squalor and ugliness and crime is a far cry from the glamorous, bewitching metropolitan city of twenty years ago. 'That was when Johannesburg was Johannesburg,' people say with undisguised pride.

When I was seventeen I knew the city as paradise where one could go and lose oneself, forgetting the drabness of the black townships. It was a city of high fashion and bustling industry. Most people over the age of thirty recall with an aching yearning the bright lights, the culture and the excitement. They shed a tear for this once classy lady who has swallowed many an innocent country bumpkin.

Johannesburg was once a haven for serious shoppers and pleasure seekers. There were the big department stores like John Orr's and Greatermans, where only the well-heeled could shop. There were magnificent hotels and expensive restaurants that were once reserved for whites only.

Even though blacks were always outside, looking in, because of apartheid laws, most people still remember it with fondness and a sense of loss.

The stock exchange building was right in the middle of town and the economy was thriving, depending which side of the racial line you were. There were theatres and museums and art galleries and culture. Johannesburg's main streets like Commissioner, Eloff, Market and Pritchard were the busiest and prettiest, lined with rows of shops that sold anything from furniture to jewellery. My sangoma principal, who is in her seventies, boasts about how she used to strut down Commissioner Street in her finest rags and turn the heads of men.

During those days men were allowed to make catcalls and admire women openly. In fact, they were expected to. Any self-respecting black woman would feel insulted if she went past a group of men and there was not a squeak from them.

As a mining town, Johannesburg had attracted all kinds of people from different parts of the world and there was a fast-paced rhythm to it. My generation enjoyed the Johannesburg of the Seventies and Eighties when the Carlton Centre was built. It was the tallest building in town, with fifty floors.

Unlike our parents, who grew up in the Fifties and were victims of the harsher colour bar, we could stroll around the

Carlton and see a movie at Ster Kinekor. We could have meals at the various restaurants if we could afford it. Apartheid was slowly crumbling. We were the generation of Black Consciousness. We sported Afro hairstyles and bell-bottomed pants. We were young and hip and were going to change the world. We raised a clenched fist at the slightest provocation.

We hung out in record bars like Look & Listen and wore clothes from Off The Peg, Smiley Blue and Truworths. Even during the turbulence of the late Seventies and Eighties when resistance to apartheid was at its height, there was an air of excitement, of wonder at taking the 17-kilometre ride from Soweto to the city of Jozibele.

Sometimes it was just to go and buy a few groceries at one of the supermarkets or meat at the butchery. At night we liked nothing better than strolling through the bright streets of the city. There were no thugs waiting to pounce; no pavements cluttered with surly street vendors. One could breathe.

Today I patronise a different Johannesburg, which could be right in the heart of the countryside. This is the Faraday Station market where all kinds of medicinal plants are on sale. It is a world of its own. A strange, fascinating and sometimes frightening world: the world of the traditional healer.

Here a medicine woman or man can find roots, herbs, animal skins and fat to heal almost any disease or condition. The atmosphere is different from any part of the city. Everything is in slow motion. You have to take your time shopping and really connect with people. There is no rushing around and grabbing articles from the shelves.

If you want to bring back an estranged lover, there are herbs and roots you can purchase. But you have to communicate honestly with the vendor and reveal your deepest secrets.

If you are having trouble finding a job there is a wide choice of medicines to help you change your luck. There is medicine to heal physical and psychological diseases. There are spells and charms that can help you weave magic. If you have the money and the knowledge, you can get bones, feathers and all kinds of powders to help you either win the lottery or get a husband or a wife.

There are inyangas and sangomas, men and women of all persuasions, to assist you. These are people who walk between the spiritual and the physical world. They have psychic powers to divine and reveal secrets. There are also just as many charlatans who will sell you the wrong muti if you are ignorant. So you have to use your intuition to know who to trust.

Some of the vendors are herbalists who operate as chemists, selling the prescribed medicine. There are those who throw the bones to tell your fortune for a small fee. They also prescribe medication.

My favourite stall in the market is Mkhize's shack. It's a makeshift house in which you can hardly swing a cat. Mkhize is a professional traditional dancer who has toured the world. He is also an inyanga. Although his name is Lawrence, he is commonly known as Romance (pronounced Lomance). His home boys from Emkhomazi in KwaZulu-Natal find it easier to pronounce Romance than Lawrence.

Romance casts out bad spells. He likes to enhance his customers' love lives. He is passionate about healing herbs and has put himself under the supervision of the best herbalists to learn his craft. He is also generous and shares this information freely. I have spent hours talking to him and learning about the art of healing.

Faraday Station Muti Market is a fascinating experience. It's a world where dreams are made; a world in which I belong.

Ruth Bhengu has been a journalist for more than twenty years. She has worked for publications in South Africa and abroad including The World, Sowetan, The Voice, Drum and Tribute. She is presently practising as a traditional healer and communications consultant.

Malay Camp and the Drill Hall

Doc Bikitsha

Before the African National Congress treason trialists landed at Drill Hall, they were linked to a rundown settlement known as Malay Camp, at the back of the Johannesburg magistrates' courts. Situated in Ferreirastown, it had more character than a shantytown or squatter camp. It had a place in the mining and colonial history of the city.

I took to it like a duck to water. Its people were the darndest in God's creation. Indians, Coloureds, Chinese, Africans and aliens. It was not far from the first black legal practice of Mandela and Tambo at Chancellor House, between West and Fox streets. You can imagine young and spruce Nelson Mandela, with parted hair, in an elegant suit, strutting to the courts, academic gown flung over his shoulder.

In my youthful folly, I considered Nelson Mandela and

Oliver Tambo arrogant and puffed up. As I matured and got to know them better, I realised they could lay their lives down for you and me. They did for the whole nation.

Not far from their offices near Bezuidenhout Street were the ANC headquarters at Macosa House. This is where the revolution was hatched, on the way to freedom and democracy! Macosa House opposite Malay Camp was a reporter's haven. It housed the ANC offices and Wilfred Sentso's typing and shorthand school.

Everybody who mattered milled about Macosa House. For me, the interest lay in the typing school: the female students. Likeable and respectable, Wilfred Sentso was a remarkable man. Apart from educational matters, he was a famous musician and leader of the vaudeville troupe, the Synco Fans. Charming, leggy ladies who performed as far as my hometown, Madubula Hall, in the Roaring Forties and early Fifties.

But it all happened around Malay Camp. The late gifted photographer Bob Gosam introduced me to the delights of Malay Camp in the Fifties. There was a swathe of pulsating shebeens and pleasure joints across the settlement. Nearby was Chinatown, where I got hooked on Chinese fried duck called Sukhai. I also tried a pipe of opium. Bob advised me: 'Lie down and go ahead. It will save you the indignity of falling down like an imploding building.'

I was also introduced in Malay Camp to a brew called Budweiser by two buddies from Chicago (the Munsieville township in Krugersdorp, where Desmond Tutu grew up). Later I discovered it was a mixture of orange juice with a liquid from a container labelled 'Carbon Tetrachloride'. (No offence to American Budweiser.) It was like another lethal concoction from the former Jan Smuts Airport called Ai-Ai. The first reduced able-bodied and seasoned drinkers to crawling, slobbering idiots. The second, a mixture of jet fuel and fruit cordial, blinded and rendered its drinkers incontinent. Others died overnight, depending on the dosage. By the grace of the devil, some of us survived.

Malay Camp fed and quenched thousands of people from the courts. Lawyers, cops, pimps, touts and thugs cracked bottles and broke bread together. There was no class distinction – one of the tenets of the Freedom Charter. Residents of Malay Camp were fascinating. A shebeener, Bra Zacks, owned a fishing boat in False Bay and brought back fresh snoek. There was Ms Fatti Lee a Chinese lady who provided journalists with drinks and fags on tick when their funds dried up. She was an institution. Popular amongst *Drum* and *Golden City Post* journalists was a shebeen called 'The Church'. (There was a Bethany Chapel nearby.) It was here that the late, inimitable Can Themba held court and we rookies listened spellbound to veteran sports editor, the late Sy 'Steeplechase' Mogapi, and to the Pan Africanist Congress firebrand, Matthew Nkoane.

A little further away was the Drill Hall, between Pritchard and Claim streets. Recently a part of it was demolished, despite its being a historic landmark associated with the colonial past of Jozi. In its heydays, the Drill Hall accommodated several military regiments and battalions.

But it assumed more fame when its main hall was converted into a courtroom in 1956, to try Nelson Mandela and a hundred and fifty-five others for treason. I covered the trial with renowned author Es'kia Mphahlele, who was literary editor of *Drum*. He did nothing but read for his Master's degree, which he passed with distinction. But he often glanced through my notebook in court for his articles. *Drum* was yellow and only used the dramatic evidence.

The Treason Trial was unique and made international headlines. The trialists were cooped up in a huge steel and mesh wire cage. Far from boring, the trial evoked lots of laughter and camaraderie, which made me clash with the Afrikaner court orderly who reprimanded me for laughing as if I was in a 'bioskoop'. He also nicked me several times stealing a sip from my concealed half-jack of doctored brandy called Korea or Mickey Finn. My paper, *Bantu World*, had thrown me into the deep end with this trial. I was a rookie and bandied words with court officials in my ignorance.

There were many more pleasant memories about the Drill Hall. But with the passing of time, this edifice turned into a derelict shell housing the poor and homeless. A squatter camp, later gutted by a fire. When I watched bulldozers bringing down the arched facade of the building on television, I felt sad. I would not mind a brick or two from the rubble as memorabilia. Because of my disgusting habit of dumping empty bottles of grog anywhere, somebody may retrieve something of my memorabilia near the armoury, lockers and ablution block. Those were my favourite dump sites.

I once chanced upon an exercise session at Union Park nearby, where soldiers drilled. I lingered long enough to polish off a nip of Korea, my rotgut brandy, when something caught my eye. A few soldiers, rookies, had collided on turning. What makes some turn left, when the command is right? Why do they concertina into each other when ordered to halt? It became a regular source of merriment as I did my rounds. They were a marvel to watch at passing out parades. Those blundering rookies became precision machines. We cheered and I slugged my prohibited liquor in celebration.

All that is gone: Drill Hall, Malay Camp and Union Park. I don't mean the structures, but the spirit. The memories remain. When I was asked to write about Jozi, city of many names, I agreed with a chuckle. Malay Camp was demolished long ago. Gone is the 'Church' and the Xhosa woman's stall where Mandela and Tambo, two rustics, used to find traditional food at lunchtime. Tambo loved ice cream, even in winter. He would often be slurping on his cone in Malay Camp. Fatti Lee . . . I don't know. All that remains now are parking lots and business premises. Macosa House still stands, and when I was last there, an oriental business was selling fans,

toys, tourist fads and a popular aphrodisiac – or tiger balm –
called Pien Tong, the 'brush'.

**Doc's full name is Sipho Neo Bridgeman Basil Bikitsha, but he
is known as Doc or Carcass. He has been around for more than
seven decades and remembers when Oliver Tambo and Nelson
Mandela came to Johannesburg as country bumpkins. He lives
in Randfontein, which he calls AWB territory, after a party of
extreme right-wingers. He is recovering from the effects of the
brews mentioned in his story.**

A quick tour around contemporary Johannesburg

Lindsay Bremner

A new, multimillion, award-winning building houses the head office of ABSA, one of South Africa's biggest banks. Its three, sky-linked office towers contain a number of atria in which staff do their shopping, visit the hairdresser, weigh in at the clinic, work out at the gym, take lunch in the staff canteen or sip coffee in a coffee shop fronting the street. After work, taxis and buses stop outside the front door and freeway access is close by. It might as well be anywhere for all it has to do with the multicultural muddle around it.

Other large corporations have similarly dug in. They have carved the city into patrolled, flag-festooned, designer-paved precincts known as Community Improvement Districts. All the activities that usually make a city thrive – coffee shops, magazine stands, bookstalls, stationers, chemists, travel agents, florists, hairdressers, have relocated into these corporate enclaves. For those inside, the city has ceased to exist. For those outside, it is a rather sad world of former retail space now bricked up, demolished buildings, open parking lots, vacant office space and slow street trade. Small cash lenders, wholesale hawker outlets, public phone shops and cheap fast food stores service the city's poor. For those not at the bottom of the economic pile nor enclosed in a corporate cocoon, downtown Johannesburg is a rather awkward place to be.

Which is why many of its citizens no longer have a sense of belonging in Johannesburg at all. They live, work and play in the suburbs. While they still speak fondly of Jozi, it is no longer a central or important figure in their collective landscape. Their experience of the city is shadowy, masked by a disdain for the urban (and love of the suburbs), a deep fear of the heterogeneous and a horror of middle age – all qualities of downtown Johannesburg. The Johannesburg to which most people aspire is the homogeneous shopping malls and Tuscan-styled villas in the city's northern suburbs. Downtown lies outside the frame.

Melrose Arch, a still-under-construction development just north of the city centre, has been designed to appeal to this new suburban citizen. It ripped up one of the city's oldest residential suburbs to create a premixed design package of flashy offices, penthouses, shops, a hotel, health club, theatre, car showroom and a public square – the perfect lifestyle package for an aspiring cosmopolitan. People are moving in before the paint is dry.

Important to its success is its allusion to the traditional city. Its intimate streets, small-scale facades, village square, lamp-posts, bollards, trees and benches create the illusion of a suburban main street, conjuring up an emotionally satisfying image of bygone times. It is the city as we wish it were, represented as an idealised fragment of what it was, accessible only to those with a great deal of disposable income. It all feels rather uncomfortably, upmarket-ly fake. Walking around Melrose Arch feels like being a tourist in your own town.

Which is also what it feels like – though for very different reasons – to visit the Apartheid Museum located to the south of the city centre. This building is wrapped in a fortress-like ten-metre high stone wall. Its cavernous exhibition spaces are buried under an artificially constructed, sloping mound of earth. Its poetry constructs a neutral, abstract space in which the full brutality of apartheid is powerfully conveyed. At once traumatic, shocking and bewilderingly absurd, these spaces resist, not only this city's tendency to trivialise everything, but also the ease with which it chooses to forget.

Under construction at much the same time as the Apartheid Museum was another interior world, Montecasino, the Tuscan-styled gambling citadel in Johannesburg's northern suburbs. Motivated not by the social obligation to remember, but by the commercial imperative to forget, this authentically fake ornamental interior is now rated one of the top ten casinos in the world. It wraps us in a fun-filled, never-ending twilit utopia, where the pigeons don't shit and the roofs cast shadows on the sky. Underwear hangs above its streets and flags following the fortunes of the teams in the Italian soccer league are draped in its piazzas. Its simulation is so perfect, it is, for some, infinitely better than the real thing.

A stone's throw from Montecasino lies prestigious Fourways Gardens residential estate, where people pay a lot of money to come home to a secured, suburban version of the African bush. Its curving streets are planted with different indigenous trees and named after them. It boasts clipped verges, cobbled crossings, an immaculate park along a watercourse and a nature reserve stocked with small buck, birds and a breeding zebra couple.

This tamed, suburban bush has broad appeal, particularly to American expatriates, who occupy roughly half of its 920 properties. Here the Fourth of July is celebrated with Elvis lookalikes, Cadillacs and hot dogs. Halloween and Thanksgiving are bigger than Youth or Freedom Day, and estate flags were flown at half mast for September 11th.

All of these scenic enclaves – Fourways Gardens' America in the bush, Montecasino's Tuscan hill town, Melrose Arch's Main Street, and parts of downtown – do the same thing. They hollow out parts of the city and, on the basis of idealised images, construct urban places appealing to the desire, nostalgia or paranoia of people who can pay to be there. None of them have much, if any, connection to the rest of the city or its history. The city is remade as a collection of juxtaposed fragments, its past confined, ossified in the silent halls of the museum to apartheid.

Maybe, at the end of the day, we are still just a mining town after all. Where most of the people live out-of-sight lives in appalling conditions so that some of the people can get rich quick; where people don't plant things in the earth and watch them grow, but stake their claim, exploit its wealth, and move on. Perhaps, despite all attempts to reconfigure our economy, our politics, our society and our city, it is this unconscious history of self-interested indifference that will continue to shape Johannesburg's future.

Lindsay Bremner is Chair of Architecture at the University of the Witwatersrand, Johannesburg. She was recently awarded the Bessie Head Fellowship by the *Sunday Times* for her essays, *Contemporary Johannesburg: Cultures, Spaces, Identities*. She has lectured in South Africa, Europe, the Middle East and Latin America and has published widely on architecture and the city.

Sport and Cars

Darrel Bristow-Bovey

There are only two things that men in Johannesburg care about: sport and their cars. Actually, that is not true. There are other things we care about, such as sex and money and when the hell they are going to stop digging up all the roads that lead out of Sandton. But mainly we care about sport and our cars, and that is very convenient, as the story I shall tell is about sport and cars. It is also about trust and fear and prejudice, but mainly it is about sport and cars.

My good friend Chunko was visiting from Cape Town. Two things happen when friends visit from Cape Town. The first thing is that an unconscionable amount of beer gets spilled. The second thing is that I become a Johannesburg man. Johannesburg men are forever displaying their manhood. When we are together with other Johannesburg men it is not so bad – we have seen each other's manhood so many times the novelty has worn off – but in the presence of Capetonians our chests puff and our jaws jut and we swagger like John Wayne wearing heels of unequal height.

'The difference between Cape Town men and Johannesburg men,' I frequently explain, 'besides the fact that we make more money and most of us are heterosexual, is that we know how to survive in a big city.' To which Chunko replies: 'Well, if you're making so much money, you won't mind picking up this round, then.' Which tells me that Cape Town men are crafty, and have selective hearing.

So Chunko was in town, and we had tickets to watch Bafana Bafana play France. The match was downtown, at the FNB stadium. I had never been to the FNB stadium at night. I had seldom been downtown at all. Frightening stories get told in Johannesburg about what goes on downtown. Apparently monsters live there. There are dragons and tar pits and, I don't know, giant clams that close around your ankles. As we drove south along the M1, singing insulting football songs, Chunko began to cast shifty glances at the darkening city. 'So you know the way, and everything, right?' he said.

There is nothing that brings out the Johannesburg man more than a Cape Town man showing fear. 'Ho ho,' I scoffed. 'You're in safe hands, my friend. Just do as I do.' An hour later, as we twisted through the scurrying streets, trying to find our way to the distant stands and floodlights, Chunko was becoming increasingly twitchy. 'I'm trying to do as you do,' he said in an unpleasant tone of voice, 'but I can't get that dimwit look just right.'

Eventually we found the stadium. It was surrounded by parked cars. It was as though a passing thunderstorm had dropped cars instead of water. There were cars everywhere. There were puddles of cars. There were new cars and old cars and cars that looked like they had been towed to the stadium as a practical joke. There were too many cars. As I drove I noticed rows of likely fellows leaning against walls, inspecting the vehicles through narrowed eyes. You expected them to be picking their teeth with snapped-off car aerials.

'The game is going to start,' whined Chunko.

'Then get out and go inside while I find somewhere to park,' I said through clenched teeth.

'I'm not going out there on my own,' said Chunko.

Finally, down a side alley, between narrow walls sprayed with rude and threatening phrases, I saw a man waving me in. I pulled up and we jumped out. I slammed the door. I looked in through the rolled-up window. My car keys dangled from the ignition.

The man grinned at me with teeth like needles. 'Don't worry,' he said. 'I will look after your car.'

I dialled the AA on my cellphone. 'The match is about to start,' Chunko whined again.

'You go to the game,' said the man with the pointy teeth. 'We will wait for the AA.' A couple of dim shapes emerged from the shadows behind him. 'Yes,' they said, 'we will watch your car.'

I looked at Chunko. 'To hell with it,' I said. 'Let's go to the game.'

So we went to the game, and it was wonderful. The night was warm and blue with the smoke of grilled chicken and chops. All around us people sang – each person a different song – and blew those horns that make a sound like a tugboat falling off the edge of the world. We swayed and we bopped and we took deep sips from whatever was inside the Liquifruit carton that the man in the yellow miner's helmet kept passing down the row.

We were the only white people there. The man in the yellow miner's helmet slapped us on the back. 'You must be French,' he said. 'Don't worry, you can wave the French flag here. You can wave any flag you like. This is not France.'

The game ended in a draw. We debated whether it was worth going back to where we had left the car. 'We will never see that car again,' I said. We decided to take a look anyway.

As we entered the alleyway, Chunko slipped his wallet into his underwear. We rounded the bend. My car was there. Three men stood around it, one leaning against the door. As we appeared he straightened and stepped towards us.

'The AA never came,' he said. 'They are too scared to come around here.'

He held out a hand. Inside his hand were my car keys. I looked at my car. It was shut and sealed tight. He winked and handed me the keys.

As we were about to drive away, he came up to my window. 'Was it a good game?' he asked.

'Yeah,' I said. 'Yeah. We played well.'

He sighed and stood upright. 'Hey, Bafana Bafana,' he said. 'You can never tell. Sometimes they are shit. Sometimes they are good. What can you do?'

'What can you do,' I agreed.

Darrel Bristow-Bovey was born in Durban, educated in Cape Town, and is currently growing up in Johannesburg. He has studied law and worked in the publishing industry but (after a brief and unhappy spell as a professional kick-boxer) now makes a living as a print and radio columnist. His most recent book was I *Moved Your Cheese*.

The Oak Tree

Tim Butcher

The box of Dutch acorns was well looked after on the long voyage south in 1852. Sixteen-year-old Hendrick Herholdt paid close attention to his grandfather's advice as he left his birthplace near Utrecht for a new life at the foot of Africa. The old man's lifework was as a woodsman, pollarding oaks as windbreaks on reclaimed fenland. There was nothing the old man did not know about oaks.

Hendrick spent long hours in the hold of the steamship that was carrying his family south. In the Atlantic's heavy spring storms he oiled the canvas lining of the box to stop the acorns from being pickled in salt water. And in the heat of the doldrums he oiled it again to stop them drying out.

The teenager had looked forward greatly to the ship's arrival in Table Bay but his father was in no mood for dawdling. The Dutch had settled Cape Town two hundred years earlier and Mr Herholdt saw the crowded and chaotic port as nothing but a staging post on his family's trek into the African interior.

For thirty years groups of Dutchmen had been claiming the land north from Cape Town. Mr Herholdt knew his family would have to travel hundreds of miles before reaching unclaimed territory. Late one summer's day in 1853 they patiently took their place in an unwieldy convoy of ox-wagons heading north.

Experience had shown winter was the only time to cross the vast rocky, desert plain of the Karoo. The days were bright and dry and the nights cold, as the convoy picked its way deeper and deeper into Africa, through hills, ravines and dry river beds. As he walked slowly alongside the wagons Hendrick would dream of home. He had brought the acorns to plant a forest that would remind him of Utrecht, a piece of Holland in Africa. But as desert stretched out for mile after mile Hendrick worried. 'Will I ever find a place with enough water to grow my trees?'

After eight months and nine hundred miles Mr Herholdt found what he was looking for; a piece of empty, unclaimed land on a north-facing ridge, well fed by streams. So plentiful were the streams during the spring storms the Dutch called it White Waters Ridge or Witwatersrand. Scrub and grass covered the rocky flanks but there were no trees. Hendrick planted the acorns and tended them through their first fragile years. More than a dozen took root but from the very beginning there was one that did better than the others. It might have been the soil, or its shaded position below a gorge, but it grew well. The young man would spend days exploring the ridge. He found rock paintings and circles of stone that had been used as cattle pens. But of these original African inhabitants, there was no further sign.

Twenty years after their arrival, the Rush began. Gold was found on the ridge's south side on a neighbour's land and things were never the same. The area became swamped with miners, chancers, traders and dealers. They looked for gold on the north but found nothing, a blessing for Hendrick's oak trees. They would have been burnt for firewood by some of the tens of thousands of new inhabitants of a mining settlement already being referred to as Johannesburg.

Hendrick survived just long enough to see the value of his family farm grow. Shortly before he died his beloved oak trees had a scare. Miners came looking for wood to be used as pit props but they turned their noses up at the short, stocky oak trees. Better pit props came from the fast-growing eucalyptus brought to the ridge by enterprising diggers from Australia.

Hendrick sold his land to an Irishman, one of the first Rand-lords, Edwardian entrepreneurs who came with nothing but who grew wealthy on the gross profits of the gold mines now dotting the southern side of the ridge. Black Africans flocked to work the mines despite the slave wages and grim working conditions.

Plots of land on the north of the ridge, away from the teeming, malodorous mining plots, were worth a fortune. It was there that tycoons built mansions, castles and estates. Hendrick's oak had matured so the Irishman was careful to use it as the centrepiece of a vast garden courtyard. Visitors would use a mounting block beneath its wide canopy and comment on how much it reminded them of home.

In the 1920s the Irishman was offered a sum he could not refuse to turn the land into the playground of the wealthy. The Johannesburg Country Club was born and with it an endless cycle of cricket matches, family functions and grand meals. The club was unashamedly British and the Old Oak, as it became known, played its part.

A vast picnic was held in its shade in 1947 when the King of England toured by train the country that had become known as South Africa. The following year club members drank gin and tonics under the tree and shook their heads as the National Party won power on a ticket of apartheid. The Britons enjoyed a life of privilege built largely on profits from the exploitation of black workers; but they balked at a racial ideology.

Black workers had cared for the oak through its life. Generations of farmhands had tended it with skill and care from storm damage, lightning strikes and insect attack. The oak was non-indigenous to Africa, an alien, an outsider, but they liked its size, stature and the speed with which it put down strong roots. When apartheid ended there were calls to rid South Africa of all alien trees that experts said were squeezing life out of indigenous plants. The chief gardener at the Johannesburg Country Club was asked if he thought the Old Oak should be cut down.

'It is part of our land now. It is mature. It provides birds with homes and guests with pleasure. It would be wrong to kill it just because it is an outsider,' was his wise view.

Tim Butcher is the Africa correspondent for the *Daily Telegraph*. His office is a short distance from the Johannesburg Country Club. Before Africa, he worked as the paper's defence correspondent, covering the Balkan war, the Middle East and North Africa. He likes trees very much.

City of restless sleep

Dave Chislett

Four am false dawn from the indigo blue of the Standard Bank sign outside the bistro. Passing cars have a bubble of silver membrane shielding them from the coming day. Looking out on to street level and all I can see are open parking bays like gaps in some street kid's teeth. Gaping oddly, not usual, needing filling. I shrug.

This place never shuts. The shaven-headed waiter nods at me as I enter. He knows what to bring. Forty-five seconds later he puts a Carling Black Label down in front of me. Cold, with advertising standard condensation trickling down its dusky flanks.

'Howzit!' he greets me, hunkering down beside my table for a while.

'Shot bru, no cool, good to see you.'

'Schweet,' he says. 'See anything good tonite?'

I laugh, thinking of the three, debut bands I saw on stage.

'Ag no, just the normal kak hey, nothing new or anything.'

'Ahh well.' He laughs too. 'Plate of nachos, hey?'

'As always.' I acknowledge with a tip of the bottle of beer.

'Schweet. Coming up.'

He disappears back into the gloomy depths of the kitchen. The bistro that never sleeps. Catz Pyjamas. Nachos and mozzarella fingers with beer at 4 am. Or full breakfasts and then some.

The ultra fake pre-dawn light of the Standard Bank neon sign is starting to make way for the slightest of hints of the real thing. The summer sun is eager to get back into the sky. For the life of me I can't figure out why. Keen to return to the scene of pollution, of dirt that makes up greater Johannesburg in the summer? Bru, I'd rather be in Cape Town!

More members of the early morning patrol ooze through the door of the bistro. Leather-clad Goths from the big Goth Industrial party at the Warehouse, ravers complete with backpacks and water pistols, well-dreaded Rastas, some alcoholic men of indeterminate age, race or creed slump in a corner, stirring only enough not to get thrown out, to order another beer.

The nachos arrive. Some kind of private sacrament for making it to 4 am, ensuring I get through to the sunrise. The waiter removes the empty beer, comes back with a refill straight away.

After a long night of beer, tequila shooters, yelled conversations in too-loud nightclubs, dancing and schmoozing, the solid greasy nature of the corn chips, guacamole and cheese is manna. Sealing the vat of my indulgence to ferment a fine vintage of hangover for later today.

Finished, I pay, smile goodbye, slide carefully into the crisp dawning air. Still dark, but you can see the light coming, just strong enough to silhouette the nearby buildings against a lighter black that is not quite grey. I stop and stare for moment. The illegal immigrant guarding my car against any thief brave enough to be abroad at this hour breaks my reverie.

'Ey Golly. Golly golly golly. What a place, hey? Egoli.'

I drive off with him berating the world for something or other, trying to get his head around Johannesburg.

I drive west, toward Aasvoëlkop, the koppie that overlooks the north-western suburbs of Johannesburg. It is amazing how much traffic there is on a road at 5 o'clock in the morning, headlights all glowing gently against the stiff competition that the dawning sun is offering.

I am single-minded, thread fast around the S bends and the hairpin turns towards the koppie until I can park my car. I climb the last couple of metres and perch on a rock to watch Johannesburg light up before my drink-riven, sleep-deprived eyes.

What a beautiful sight. Looking north, the spires and blocks of international hotels compete with giant shopping malls and office blocks. Looking south to the city centre, I see the Hillbrow tower, the clump of downtown Johannesburg huddled together, still in darkness.

What a thankless, heartless place it is, stretched out like a fat concrete cat to catch the first rays of sun. It makes my heart race and I am glad to be one of the germs that course in its blood system.

The light, once established, crashes into the valley that comprises the city, and I am very quickly a vampire caught in the sun, not the watcher coolly observing the coming dawn. I shade my eyes, duck back down and away from the glare, and notice four or five other people or groups perched among the rocks, looking out over their city. Nursing joints, beers, bottle of champagne. One or two have been crying, one or two seem too transfixed to move. Our eyes do not meet. I head to my car, they to theirs. We file one by one off the hill and into the winding roads that feed it.

It is not until I am deeply sunglassed in the Wednesday morning 7 am rush hour traffic that I realise exactly how drunk

I really still am. And then it is a straight-faced, straight-armed drive home to fall asleep to the droning lullaby of the all-purposeful worker bees that fuel this great mass of city while I cook up some more germs and wild sprees in my dreams.

Dave Chislett is a writer, journalist, babbler and promoter who was fertilised by the dusts of Johannesburg. He now applies his cynicism to living in Cape Town while trying to find time to write a novel about living in Johannesburg. Go figure.

Horizontal City: Notes on Johannesburg while in Los Angeles

Shaun de Waal

1. Flyover

Driving to the airport on the highway: thinking of LA with its highways, or rather freeways, its flyovers – is that the word?

2. Flat

In LA, someone says it's a horizontal city . . . Jo'burg is too. But LA has mountains not far away, and the Hollywood Hills to the north of the city itself, leaning into the city bowl. And the sea is nearby too. It can take a while to get to the sea, though – everything is so spread out in LA. Driving along Santa Monica Boulevard, from Santa Monica (at the coast) to West Hollywood, it's like ten miles (what's that in kilometres?)

of Louis Botha Avenue, except it's straighter. Smallish shops, storefronts; and traffic light upon traffic light. It's slower than taking the freeway, going this route, but it's easier to remember – and getting on and off the freeway is a nightmare, even proleptically, for someone used to driving on the other side of the road, someone using a map-book from 1988 (though the main roads are of course still there), let alone someone driving a Beetle *nogal*. Huge SUVs (that's American for a 4x4, and they all seem to have one) sweep past; I feel dwarfed. I feel as though people are laughing at me.

3. Why here?
I can't find out why LA is here, in this precise place. Should look it up. I know it started with a Catholic mission station, a cross between a church and a fortress, like those NGK churches in South Africa. But why here? Did it just grow from the movie industry? There are no physical features in the landscape that would invite a large city here; the city itself is not close to the sea. We know why Jo'burg is where it is, in a place without a river, and not beside the sea: gold.

4. Expansion
Jo'burg, it is often mentioned, is the biggest and most important city in the world not built on the sea or a navigable river. (LA has a river, but it's a small, insignificant one – and its beds and banks were concreted over by the state, early in the city's history, mostly to improve the value of the real estate along its banks. Now it's just a sludgy algae'd trickle, though when it floods it floods dangerously.) Jo'burg is not at the sea, and there is no river. And it is, too, a horizontal city, one that expands outward, ever outward, across the plateau that seems to stretch all the way to the Congo Basin.

5. Up/down
Yet Jo'burg is not simply horizontal; it is not just flat. It has

its topography, its ups and downs, its protrusions and declivities. Maybe I overestimate them because I want some variation in the minor altitudes of the city; it's not Cape Town, after all, with its precipitous hillsides, its Kloof Neks that rise and open to a vista of the Atlantic. But I love Jo'burg's ups and downs. I love Munro Drive and Sylvia's Pass, if it is a pass: is it a pass? I even feel a bit of a thrill just driving from Parkview, from down in the riverine valley, up towards the minor hilltop of Rosebank.

6. Riverroads

And I love the roads that curve. Munro Drive, Sylvia's Pass; the way Jan Smuts Avenue snakes its way from Braamfontein to the north. (David Hockney says he loves LA's Mulholland Drive because it's 'wiggly' when the rest of the city is a city's best attempt at a rectilinear grid.) I even like the way the highway, the M1, the Jo'burg freeway, curls around the city, coming south, if you're going south, from the direction of Pretoria, swings through Braamfontein, and shapes itself around the city centre. It feels like a great big river, Jo'burg's concrete Congo.

Shaun de Waal is book editor and movie reviewer for the Mail & Guardian. **His collection of short fiction,** These Things Happen, **was published in 1996; his graphic novelette** Jackmarks **was published in 1998.**

Turning Points

Carolyn Dempster

I never saw the hat. It belonged to my great-grandmother, a feisty Irish midwife, and it had a bullet hole straight through it.

The year was 1922. The gold miners, among them my great-uncles Tom, John and Willy, were busy digging trenches to fend off the soldiers dispatched by General Jan Smuts to put down the strike. For several years white miners had been resisting the employment of unskilled black workers on the mines, fearing the loss of their own jobs and status. Some of the strikers were socialists, some purely racists. The Rand Revolt was their last united stand, an armed rebellion which the government moved swiftly and brutally to suppress. Martial law had been declared, the army was sent in to shell the miners' positions and the streets of central Johannesburg were definitely not safe.

Nonetheless Sister Agnes Browning had a baby to deliver.

And so she made her way from her small midwifery in Fordsburg across the lines of the striking miners and police sharpshooters. As she popped her head around the corner of a building on Market Square to see if it was safe to cross, a bullet zipped through the top of her sedate black bonnet. The style in Johannesburg in those days was six inches or higher off the head. It probably saved her life.

In 1940 my father, Michael John Findlay Dempster, stepped off the boat en route from India to England. His mission: to assess the potential for setting up a South African branch of his company, Morgan Crucible. He was young, charming and good looking, a commodity rarer than gold in Johannesburg in the early days of the Second World War when most of the city's eligible men had already joined up. My father was excluded from battle because he had only one leg. The other had been amputated after a shooting accident at the age of nineteen. And so it was he found himself among a small select group of bachelors in the city.

His interest in amateur dramatics led him to the Johannesburg Repertory Players, and he was selected to play opposite my mother, Nancy Maudsley, in a production directed by Muriel Alexander, after whom the Alexander Theatre in Braamfontein was named.

The stage was set, a match was made, and my father stayed in Johannesburg. 1958 was the year I was born, coinciding with the ongoing Treason Trial of Nelson Mandela and others in the old Johannesburg Drill Hall and the election of Hendrik Verwoerd, the architect of apartheid, as Prime Minister. In his new role, one of Verwoerd's many tasks was opening the Rand Show – since 1894 the biggest agricultural and trade fair in the country. The ceremony involved releasing a batch of pigeons into the air, but according to the story told by my mother with a chuckle, Verwoerd's white pigeon flopped to the ground and walked away. The bird simply wouldn't fly, an event widely relished in the racially divided city for its symbolism.

In 1962 my father suffered a change in fortunes which resulted in him studying Afrikaans furiously for six months to qualify for a new position, that of senior design lighting engineer with the Johannesburg Municipality. No civil servant was employed who wasn't fluent in Afrikaans, one of the many laws introduced by the National Party government.

As a child I used to accompany him at night to the Simmer and Jack gold mine dumps on the edges of the city where I would sit watching him taking light meter readings and listen to the swish of the cars flashing past below me, their lights glinting off the golden residue of the dumps. Today, every time I take the Golden Highway out to Soweto, or drive south to Durban, at that precise point where the N3 sweeps around to join the N12 and intersects the M2 before it plunges into the heart of the city, the lights he designed illuminate my path.

It was a quiet Saturday afternoon in 1971 in our whites-only suburb of Hurlingham, but there were still quite a few black people strolling the streets. Most were domestic workers and gardeners. Hurlingham was where the black 'Rhodesian' immigrants had chosen to try and find work. Some were fortunate enough to have secured pass books with the support of their white 'madams', permitting them to stay in the suburb, but the vast majority had no legal papers. When the small yellow police van carrying the white policemen turned into the area that afternoon on a pass book raid, the news quickly contaminated the suburb.

Godfrey, who worked for our next-door neighbour, didn't have a pass book. Terrified at the prospect of being arrested, beaten up and then deported, he panicked and ran. He leaped over our garden fence and hid in the basement of our neighbour's house. The cops came into our garden in hot pursuit. At the age of thirteen, I lied and pointed them in the opposite direction, in the hope it would save Godfrey. They couldn't find him, but in a state of sheer terror, he jumped clean through a plate glass window to escape from his basement hiding place, slicing his face badly.

He wouldn't go to hospital for fear of arrest. And so, dripping blood on to the sienna-coloured concrete floor of our backyard, my sister Laurian, then newly qualified as a doctor, stitched up his gaping wound.

It was a taste of what she was to face subsequently at Baragwanath, the biggest hospital in the southern hemisphere, built for the burgeoning black population of Soweto.

1976 was my first year at the University of the Witwatersrand, and Laurian was working as a medical officer at Diepkloof clinic in Soweto when the black school pupils took to the streets in June in protest over the enforced use of Afrikaans as a medium of instruction in the schools. The protest quickly turned bloody as police opened fire on the youngsters, using live ammunition. My sister, who was accustomed to driving through the township to avoid the traffic and was seven months pregnant, was advised she should leave that afternoon via the most direct route. In the ensuing days, the clinics were closed. While helicopters whirled overhead, patients and students injured in the clashes had to find their own transport to Baragwanath where only the most critical cases were admitted for treatment.

My own blooding came in 1981 as a journalist for *The Star*, the descendant of the *Eastern Star*, one of the first newspapers to be published in Johannesburg. As education reporter, I was dispatched to cover a school boycott in the coloured townships of Eldorado Park and Riverlea, fringing Johannesburg. It was here that I encountered Brigadier 'Rooi Rus' Swanepoel. His nickname derived from his notorious reputation as a security policeman adept at torturing and extracting confessions from suspected members of the banned Communist Party. But in the coloured townships he adopted another role, that of terrorising children.

The boycott had been sparked by the arrest and detention

of a student leader, Aziz Jardine. His fellow pupils staged a sit-in protest and when the riot police arrived, the school-children refused to disperse. So the police locked the pupils into their first floor classrooms, threw teargas canisters into the rooms, and then set their dogs on to those students who broke the windows and slid down the outer walls to escape the choking fumes. The bloody trail of fingerprint marks down the side of the school building bore silent witness to what had happened. I rushed back to the newsroom, where I was told the story warranted only a few paragraphs.

Another small turning point in the ongoing saga of the city my family calls home.

Carolyn Dempster is a freelance correspondent for the BBC World Service and CBC Radio.

Whoring

Andrew Donaldson

When the punctilious Sanitary Superintendent A H Bleksley arrived in Johannesburg from Kimberley in the early 1890s he found the mining town in the jerk and shudder of a wild pig rut. About ten per cent of all women above the age of fifteen were prostitutes – the vast majority of them recent immigrants from Europe lured out by the goldfields. With a view to putting a stop to such things, Bleksley conducted two surveys of local immorality. His first, published in 1895, revealed that there were ninety-seven brothels in central Johannesburg and even noted their nationality – thirty-six were French, twenty German, five Russian, two American, and so on. His second, a year later, didn't bother with nationality but revealed the number of the town's brothels had risen to one hundred and thirty-three – the sort of sex industry growth spurt the city experienced a century later in the post-apartheid *fin de siècle*.

In this regard, a British journalist once told me, Johannes-burg was quite unlike any other city in the world. 'In London, say, it's not exactly something to be proud about,' he said. 'But here men actually brag about visiting the brothel. They discuss it at the office. "Went to Little Holland last night, you know? Met some mates there, had a fantastic time, was home by ten. And you? You get up to much?" It's as if you're all overdosing on Viagra.' (Actually, what chance does Pfizer have when there's Christina, a Thai with toys? In *The Star*'s classi-fied notices, she promises: 'I can suck a mouse through a garden hose.')

Of course, much of the city's amorality, its licence, has been attributed to Johannesburg's so-called frontier mentality, a throwback to the hurly-burly lawlessness of the digger days. In perhaps more legitimate lines of work if it's not the lack of ethics, then it's the aggression that is cause for alarm. One advertising executive who was recently poached from a Johannesburg agency by Madison Avenue was told to undergo 'sensitivity training' because his steamroller pitches were too much for his New York clients. Work hard, play hard. Work harder, play harder. So it goes.

Much of this playing is done out there where the money has gone, to the northern suburbs. ('Join us every day after work,' suggests a display ad for The Lounge, an upmarket club in Sandton. 'Dress code: corporate ware [sic] – no jeans or sportswear.') Such places are perhaps worlds removed from the sordid squalor of the inner city brothels and the soulless grind of the average Hillbrow streetwalker. But then there are parts of the city that are lost forever to the lieutenants, if not the captains, of commerce in Johannesburg.

Which is probably why the raid in December 2000 and subsequent closure by police of The Ranch, arguably the city's most upmarket brothel, was greeted with a loud chorus of disapproval. Some women argued that if their husbands had to go out and get something on the side, they'd rather they did it there than pick up streetwalkers or, even worse, hit on their friends. (Some men even took their girlfriends there, a treat to see 'what the other guys got up to'.) Neighbours complained that The Ranch's brothel-keeper was a 'soft target' for corrupt police jealous of his money, an otherwise law-abiding citizen who cooperated with residents and ensured that his clients behaved themselves. Cleaners and chefs who worked there believed that vice cops should rather concern themselves with the 'far more dubious' establishments in the inner city. One even described the police action as a 'cruel blow just before Christmas' – as if a raid on a brothel was an assault on family values. The Ranch, in business for fourteen years, employed some four hundred people – whores, strippers, cooks, cleaners, barmen and related personnel and even provided on-site counselling and testing services. (Bleksley would have approved.)

Whoring in Johannesburg, if I'm to believe the comments posted on an international sex-tourism Internet site, is apparently world class. One American visitor to The Ranch echoed Bleksley's earlier concerns when he listed the nationalities of the women he found there: 'A lot of the girls are Russian/Ukrainian/Bulgarian, with a sprinkling of Thais and black South Africans.' He also pointed out that the rand was 'in the toilet (about R4.65 to US$1)' and that he'd had his pipes cleaned for 'about US$140 . . . personal recommendations: Natasha and Natalia'.

Johannesburg may not have as many brothels as it did in the 1890s. But there's no shortage of escort agencies and free-lance operators out there. For this we must thank the motor car and the cellphone.

Which brings me to the following, probably true, cautionary tale: A Cape Town businessman overnighting in Johannesburg called his wife to tell her that he was OK and that his clients were taking him out for drinks. Which was true, sort of. The next morning, his wife picked up her cellphone and saw that her husband had left her a voice message at 2 am while she was asleep. Intrigued, she played it back – and heard nothing at first, except what sounded like a party in the background. Music, laughter, glasses clinking, grunts. And then her husband's shocked voice, quite distinctly: 'Three hundred bucks! But I didn't even come . . .'

Make sure, then, that your keypad is locked when you have a lapdance. Better still, just turn the phone off completely.

Andrew Donaldson works for the *Sunday Times* of South Africa. He was born in Cape Town but raised in Johannesburg. The nearest escort agency in his part of the world is Charmant in Richmond. He says he has never been there.

On a Rock

Max du Preez

I was sitting on a rock on top of the Melville Koppies in the middle of Johannesburg the other day looking over the city and the hills to the north. Suddenly, as if in computer animation, the streets and the buildings started disappearing. A beautiful landscape unfolded in front of me – hills with magnificent wild olive, acacia and karee trees, plains and valleys covered in grass swaying in the breeze.

At the foot of the hill to my left I can see a herd of elephant tugging at tree branches. In the distance the long necks and peculiar faces of a few giraffe peer over the treeline. Below, on the banks of the crystal-clear stream, a herd of zebra mixes with eland and springbok. A rhino stands perfectly still in the shade, her baby lying almost under her stocky grey-brown body. I scan the bush for lion, but see nothing.

A sudden movement on the hill about a hundred metres away catches my eye. A family of five people, dressed in animal skins, is sitting around a fire. There is a clay pot on the coals, a man is sharpening the metal blade of his spear. This is Eden.

How far back in history did my imagination's time machine take me? It's hard to tell, because Johannesburg, with Dar es Salaam, Nairobi and Addis Ababa, is one of the world's cities with the longest history of human habitation. Certainly longer than Athens, Rome or even Cairo. I have always found it fascinating that our species congregated in these parts tens of thousands of years ago, and today it is the hub of human development in Africa south of the equator.

About twenty kilometres from downtown Johannesburg, at Sterkfontein and Kromdraai, palaeoanthropologists have found the fossil remains of our species' earliest ancestors – apelike creatures, like Little Foot, who started walking upright more than three million years ago. These hominids also sat on Melville Koppies, watching the game and looking over the plains. *Homo sapiens* eventually developed from these beings some two hundred thousand years ago: social beings with language, culture and a sense of morality, who could control fire and make tools out of stone. From these grasslands on the eastern side of Africa they populated the entire world. There are now six billion of them.

Since those early times, human beings have continuously been living in the area we started calling Johannesburg just over a century ago. At first they were scavengers, hunters and gatherers. Later they were farmers, keeping cattle and planting millet. They lived a slow life close to nature. It gave them enough time to sit around the fire and tell endless stories, to philosophise about the Creation and humankind's place on earth.

A thousand years or so ago, there were human settlements on Melville Koppies and on the hills of present-day Northcliff, reaching to Broederstroom and the Magalies Mountains. Their society was arranged in chiefdoms, and among them were artistic potters and able ironsmiths and goldsmiths. There are still traces of their existence on Melville Koppies.

My own ancestors, who had left Africa many millennia ago, came back to the Mother Continent from France, Holland and Germany three hundred and fifty years ago and gradually formed a new African tribe without links with Europe. They called their tribe after the continent – they called themselves Afrikaners. They reached the area now called Johannesburg in the mid-1800s after a trek from the Cape Colony. They were farmers, but when gold was rediscovered in Johannesburg in 1886, they also became miners and traders. They formed a republic, called Die Zuid-Afrikaanse Republiek, but were defeated by the British in 1902.

The Union of South Africa was formed in 1910 by Britain from its own two colonies and the two Boer Republics, excluding black people from national political participation. The Afrikaners' main political party won the white elections in 1948 and transformed the existing colonialist practice of separation of racial groups into a rigid ideology called apartheid. This led to four decades of dehumanisation and repression of all who did not have white skins, and eventually a fierce liberation struggle.

It was again in Greater Johannesburg, a stone's throw away from the Johannesburg International Airport, that oppressed and oppressor, those who never left Africa and those who had left but then returned to make it their home again, made a peace unique in modern history. In 1994 this led to a man who was once a young Johannesburg lawyer, but then spent twenty-seven years in jail, Nelson Mandela, becoming president of a free South Africa.

So this, to me, is Johannesburg, a living reminder of humankind's common ancestry and perpetual search for freedom and justice.

This is why every visitor from anywhere in the world can say: I am a Johannesburger. I am an African.

(Suggested reading on early African history: *The Roots of Black South Africa* by David Hammond-Tooke, Jonathan Ball Publishers, 1993; *From Lucy to Language* by Donald Johanson and Blake Edgar, Witwatersrand University Press, 1996; *The African Experience* by Roland Oliver, Pimlico, 1994.)

Max du Preez is a newspaper columnist, author and documentary film maker.

Signs of Life

Alex Duval Smith

On a car journey filled with wrong turns and bad map-reading, two journalists – one foreign and one a native of Johannesburg – attempted to rediscover the city through its signs. They started at the eastern end of Main Reef Road – which runs along the city's gold vein – and finally Arrived Alive, as journalists do, in Melville.

BOKSBURG WEST. *So we're not in Benoni, after all. R21. This will do. Rietfontein Road intersects with Main Reef Road.* Norman's Used Cars. Dick Coen Alignment Centre. Hoofrifweg. *Here we are.* R29W. Brakpan Let Yourself Go. *There's an old headgear from a mine.* Balmoral Sports Club. *That mock-Tudor building by the squatter camp was once a mining house.* Hola 7 Tuck Shop.

LILIANTON. *There's a shack built with a Telkom sign.* Nescafé:

Open Your Window And Taste Adventure. *I feel car sick.* Hein's Scrap Metals. *Would it help to open your window?* Gilly's funeral parlour. *Then we'll probably get hijacked.* R5 000 cash family funeral policies.

BURTON PARK ADVERTISE HERE. *There has never been any development here because this is wetland and the underground mining has made it unstable.* Alstom. Tomco Armature Winders: Welders and Generators. *I came here as a teenager and learned to fire a gun.* Paintball City. *With your brothers? No, my boyfriend. He collected guns.* 3 beers for 13 rands. *Beats swapping football cards.* Knights Gold Recovery Ltd. *When the gold price hit $300 they got into recovery because a lot of gold was left in the waste.* Citizen: Missing Teen Found. *I think we've lost Main Reef Road.*

GERMISTON CBD. *Gosh, Germiston's got a Central Business District.* Wag Vir Groen. Signwriter Pat. *Now it's calling itself Johann Rissikweg.* R29 *here we are!* Safe abortions, Contraceptives. Sterilisations. 0800 117785. *You think Main Reef is called R29 all the way through but it's not, you know.* Pure & Cool Roadhouse. Rent A Shed: The Shed Hire Corporation. *We're actually on Stanhope Road.* Buy and Braai. *See what I mean!* Joe Carr Agencies: Component Supplier To The Mattress Industry. 615 8232.

MALVERN. Fereiras Panel Beaters. Hotel Estoril. *Ah! A Portuguese flavour.* New York Tailors. International Restaurant. *This looks rough.* Jules Street. *Got your doors locked?* Make a comfortable deal at Mario's Pawn. *R34 995 for a Mitsubishi pickup.* Ding Gone: Hail damage specialist 615 7566. Mr Plastic has moved. Used vehicles for cash.

JEPPESTOWN. Gun safes. The J&P Pool Club where all friends meet. A1 Taxi House Finance Services. *Poor whites around here*. Gun Gloss. *Yeah, but everyone can afford a satellite dish*. Ngaka Ya Mehlo. *The Zulu hostels are near here*. John Page Drive. *This is where the Zulus gathered on the anniversary of the Shell House massacre when ANC gunmen fired on members of Inkatha Freedom Party*.

MAIN STREET. Special promotion bread R2.50. Cellphone prepaid cards. Crime Stop Armed Response. Carsons outfitters for all your family clothing needs. *Is Main Street the same as Main Reef Road?* Tommy Steele Inc 334 8727. *Same. It goes through town*. New Nugget Hotel. *It was a drinking joint for Rand Daily Mail journalists*. Rand Realty: To Let – suites from 150 sq m to 1,500 sq m, already 70% let. *Cobbled street here*. Hair Studio. *This feels like one of those surveillance camera areas*. Carlton Centre Ice Rink. *On the right is the Carlton Hotel. It used to be the smartest hotel in town. There's a plan to make it a detention centre*. Make Friends In High Places. Old Mutual Properties. Gandhi Square. *Is that a new name? Cool!* Atlas Finance: Free funeral cover, conditions apply. *I'm turning here*. Fox Street. *It says buses only*. Millew's Modes. *Ooops, cops*. Police 10111. *It's OK, they didn't notice*. Crockett & Jones: Chubb Armed Response, trespassers will be prosecuted, we are open, pull.

LOVEDAY STREET. Gun Shop. Improvement District: Safe & Clean. *Part of a regeneration scheme*. Sauer Street. *On our right are all the Anglo buildings and the Chamber of Mines. Empty?* Eerste Nasionale Bank. *Not at all*. Unite Against Aids. 0800 11 33 22. ANC Chief Albert Luthuli House. The Star *where I started in journalism*. Johannesburg Stock Exchange. *All the action at the JSE has moved to Sandton*. 11 Diagonal Street: *Diamond-shaped because it's the De Beers building*. Mohammed Musa Store: Museum Of Man And Science: The King Of Muti – herbal and homeopathic remedies. West Street. Vote ANC 5th December. *Which elections were they?*

Speeding up change and fighting poverty. *Must have been the local government elections in 2000*. Pat Mbatha Public Transportway. *We shouldn't be going under this train bridge.* metro metro metro metro metro. *I thought there wasn't a metro in Jo'burg. There isn't, yet, Sam Shilowa's express is still coming*. Pay As You Go MTN. U-turn.

PRESIDENT STREET. Oriental Plaza. *They built it in the 1970s after they removed all the Indian traders from the streets of Vrededorp*. Mohammed's Halal Takeaways. *Great shopping!* Dubai Tiles. *That's not the point*. HBZ Bank: A subsidiary of Habib Bank. Amina's dressmaking school 892 3607. Taj Palace Restaurant. Garden City 24 hr Casualty. *You can tell you're getting to the posh bits when there are signs for hospitals*. Homeless Talk. *And beggars*. Anniversary Issue. *I've got a copy already*. Central Lock. *So have I. Sorry sisi. Another time. Yes, another time, maybe*. Gold Reef City Casino (left). *I'm dying for a café latte, aren't you?*

BRIXTON. Enos Sontonga Cemetery. *He wrote the national anthem*. Citizen: Bio Hazard Truck Hijacked. *Nkosi Sikelel-i-Af-ri-ka . . .* The Star: The Cost of Kylie's Beauty *. . . Malupha-kanyiswu phondo lwayo . . .* Divorce: R900 – Vissers of West-dene Attorney *. . . Yizwa imithandazo yethu . . .* All-Guard Security Armed Reaction 673 2141 *. . . Nkosi Sikele-la!* Since When Did No Mean Yes? LoveLife. Let's Talk About It. *Talk about what? Good question*. Change, Choice, Chat, Cell C for yourself. Randse Afrikaanse Universiteit.

MELVILLE. Previously owned cars for sale. Theosophical Society. Chubb. ADT. BBR. St Peter's Church, Anglican. Qaphela Inja – Beware Of The Dog. African Renaissance Interior Design. *Now, where shall we park?* Melville Security Initiative 082 369 0234. *There's someone in a bib, waving*. Melville Pharmacy. The Bead Shop. Melville Spin Studio: Dawie is back! *That'll do*. Central Lock. Be-beep! *Hi, what's your name?* Reminiscene Vintage Period Clothing. *Emmanuel: watch this car. We'll see you later*. Today's Specials. Xai Xai Lounge. Right of admission reserved, please mind the step. Visa, American Express Cards Welcome. The Full Stop.

Alex Duval Smith is a former Africa correspondent for *The Independent*. She now lives in Paris and is writing a novel and a play.

Fringe Country

Mark Gevisser

To find Johannesburg's past I had to drive northwards, out of the city, through the endless boomed suburbs and cluster-home developments and neo-classical office parks, along thoroughfares named for Afrikaner leaders, through suburbs that evoked bucolic idylls. I had to pass the obscenity of a gargantuan casino housed in a Hollywood impression of a Tuscan hillside village, its ramparts leering over Johannesburg in a nightmarish reincarnation of the mining town's bawdy-house past, and drive through the peri-urban sprawl of light industry and squatter camps, out on to what is known as the mink-and-murder belt, where the descendants of the mining magnates built their follies, kept their horses, hoarded their treasures. At Lanseria aerodrome I had to bump down a crenellated dirt road, past cows and gumtrees and labourers' children skipping home from school in their gymslips until, my car encased in the fine ochre dust of the Highveld, I arrived at the Bailey's African Photographic Archives, on the eccentric country estate of the founder-publisher of the *Drum* empire, Jim Bailey.

Jim Bailey has since passed away and his archives have moved, finally, to town. But for years, in rooms filled in equal measure with dust and whimsy, he housed those images that have come to define black urban Johannesburg life: Nelson Mandela sparring with Jerry Moloi on a city rooftop; Dolly Rathebe in a bikini up a mine dump; Hugh Masekela and Satchmo's trumpet.

It was here, while researching my biography of Thabo Mbeki, that I happened upon a folder entitled 'No Colour Bar: 1961', buried deep in the filing cabinets. I poured its contents out on to a table, and they were a genie unbottled, the stardust of lost possibility: dozens of prints of blacks and whites boxing together, playing tennis together, acting on stage together, swimming together, helping each other across the street, arguing at art openings together, jamming together in late-nite jazz clubs. Cross-referencing the photographs to a bound volume of *Drum*, I saw that they were collected for a six-page pullout, written by the magazine's *enfant terrible*, Nat Nakasa, in the March 1961 issue, entitled 'Fringe Country, where there is no Colour Bar'. Fringe Country, declared Nakasa, was 'that social no man's land, where energetic, defiant, young people of all races live and play together as humans . . . where anybody meets anybody, to hell with the price of their false teeth, or anything else . . . Some people call it "crossing the colour line". You may call it jumping the line or wiping it clean off. Whatever you please. Those who live on the fringe have no special labels. They see it simply as LIVING. Dating a girl. Inviting a friend to lunch. Arranging a party for people who are interested in writing or painting, jazz or boxing, or even apartheid, for that matter.'

One of the photographs accompanying the text was that of a white woman and a black man horsing around in a swimming pool, above the caption, 'Where's this? Surely not South Africa, with white and black in the same swimming pool? If that's what you thought, you are wrong, this picture was taken in one of [the] smartest suburbs of white Johannesburg.' The eyes of both man and woman are closed: they are in a whirl-pool of their own making, utterly contained, held by the corruscations of the late-afternoon sun on the rippling water. What makes this photograph so brilliant an analogue of its subject material is that there is no visible physical contact between the man and the woman and yet we *know*, by the positions of their bodies and the expressions on their faces, that beneath the surface of the water they are intertwined.

In the folder of photographs there was another image of the same scene taken from a wider angle, shot just moments before the above clench. Standing in the shallow end is a coloured man, locked into solipsistic intimacy with a white woman who is sitting at the pool's edge dangling her feet into the water. Behind them, receding back to a house and a row of old sun-dappled trees, are untidy clusters of semi-naked white families, doing what white families do on a Sunday afternoon in suburban Johannesburg. All form a halo of human activity around the focal point of the photograph: a powerfully built, strikingly handsome black man, wading through the pool at nipple-level towards the white woman who will – we know, from the following photo – pull him down into the water with her.

I am a child of suburban Johannesburg. Looking at this photo I felt unutterable loss; a hunger that rippled down the sides of my tongue and gathered in my throat, for the sycamore berries and the bluegum pods beneath bare feet, caught in the grooves between the slasto paving; for the tray of lemon-barley squash and tennis biscuits on a glass-topped iron table; for the sun reflected off a zinc roof on to beds of Namaqualand daisies; for the insane, prehistoric shriek of hadeda ibises piercing the sky, the purple violence of a cloudburst, the lengthening shadows, the inevitable nightfall quick as a gangster's knife. I was born three years after these photographs were taken, just as the Rivonia trialists were beginning their life sentences on Robben Island: there were no such poolside gatherings any more. I look, now, at these photographs and see my childhood, blanched, with the focal point – that black man advancing through the water – removed. I see what might have been.

Mark Gevisser is a born-and-bred Johannesburger, author, journalist and film maker. He is currently completing a biography of Thabo Mbeki, from which the above is extracted, and writing scripts for a new TV crime series set in Johannesburg. He is Writing Fellow at the Wits Institute for Social and Economic Research (WISER).

The more things change ...

Jodie Ginsberg

When the prison on Robben Island was turned into a museum, the new owners got there to discover that someone had painted over the walls. The cramped corridors and decaying cells had been cleaned up, touched up, the finer details of apartheid painted over and out.

Nobody knows who gave the order to scrub out the prison's grimy past. But visitors to the now brightly lit island jail must settle for verbal pictures of days that were as dark as the nights.

No one has taken such trouble with room number one, 247 Rooyen Road. Eight feet square, this concrete rooftop box squats above an apartment block modestly named Buckingham Place. Long-standing residents like to call it 'The Place' but the building is hardly unique: these brick apartment blocks pack the streets of Johannesburg's wealthy northern suburbs. Their names echo that faded empire which the original residents sought to imitate with linen serviettes, silver bells at dinner, and servants' quarters: Sandringham, Hyde Park, Windsor, Earl Ridge. All boast these hidden cells – one for each main flat.

Room number one – hurried together with the bits left behind when the 'real' flats were finished – huddles with twenty other such boxes whose crumbling doors tremble on rusty hinges. Pushed back from the roof's edge, you can barely see them from The Place's perfect lawns – lizard green in the bright winter sun. Perhaps that's why no one bothered to paint the room, to cleanse it for the public.

The walls of room number one haven't nosed Johannesburg air since Buckingham Place was built half a century ago. Thick, yellowing paint like cheap nail polish cracks from the ceiling or bubbles up in sweaty corner patches. The entire room – paced in three steps – is streaked with smoke from countless paraffin stoves. It is filthiest at the edges – window-sill, doorframe, worn out by sticky hands, toughened thumbs. The putty in the windows is black and shattered so the panes shake.

Up here, there is no shelter from the wind. You feel it everywhere. Where Robben Island prisoners had bars, the skyline inhabitants get smoked glass. And like those dingy island corridors, the rooms are lit with a single sickly bulb.

There are few visitors. The occupants are maids with new titles: housekeepers, cleaners, nannies; handymen; the gardener. Each is handed a single key by an employer downstairs, and then disappears. This rooftop residence is another time, another place, built to stay out of sight and out of mind: the building's lift stops at the floor below. Visitors to room number one must go the last part of the way up raw concrete stairs, then walk the length of the building along an unlit, uncovered walkway shattered by fifty years of Johannesburg weather.

There is no security in these invisible homes. Downstairs, tenants cosy themselves behind steel gates, two locks in solid oak doors, a chain. Up here, the shit-brown door of room number one has been crowbarred open more than once. A tiny padlock pulls the door to but the gesture is purely symbolic – everyone knows the man in number two can open it with a single kick.

Room number two has a television. The guy has somehow managed to hook up power from the overhead lines. He's got a heater, radio, electric cooker – no paraffin stove to streak his walls. But electricity costs money. And while nobody has ever thought to wire these rooms, The Place's tenants committee – long-timers who cherish their silver dinner bells and whose daily grind is preserving the 'tone' of the building – is thoughtful enough to charge all roof residents a flat rate. They say this covers the few who are brave enough to 'arrange' their own supply and, after all, there have been no accidents yet.

One of the tenants is looking for furniture for room number one. There are plenty of bargains to be had in this building – the old ladies are tripping over themselves to leave Jo'burg for safer places: New York, Washington DC, north London. The latest émigré has beautiful pieces: delicate Art Deco lounge suites, silk cushions, a formidable carved bedstead. She grabs the young man's arm and confesses in a stage whisper that she won't sell any of it to blacks because 'they'll break it'. For a moment, the would-be purchaser thinks Blacks is a furniture store.

It won't take much to furnish room number one, though. A single bed, a small table, somewhere to put the stove. There is no sink, no tap. The unseen inhabitants share two bathrooms. They keep them clean, but cannot eradicate the peppery mould that claws its way from floor to ceiling.

This is Johannesburg, 2002. Former prisoners now escort wide-eyed tourists round Robben Island, point out the whitewashed walls, their old cells, the quarries where they were forced to work. The soon-to-be occupant of room number one is also returning to her old workplace. Her previous employer, falling over herself to get out of the country, died. For now, she is staying with her mother – room number seven. But soon she will start the old routine in a new cell. She is my maid.

Jodie Ginsberg is a correspondent for Reuters news agency. She is based in Johannesburg.

Tea and cake at the
Johannesburg Public Library

Stephen Gray

For years on end, this was my monthly routine: attending a meeting of the Consultative Committee of the downtown Johannesburg Public Library. I had been elected on to the committee as a replacement for some old codger in 1983.

Soon I gathered that the committee's brief was to add a certain moral firmness to the decisions of the admirable and brave lady librarians in their selection of the monthly booklist. Nor was I averse to spending a few million rands every so often on the latest books and periodicals in the field in which I could hardly otherwise say I specialised.

But our first duty was, if they ran into any difficulty over a politically sensitive book with the apartheid censors, to raise a sustained and ongoing outcry of distinguished male citizens from across the disciplines, letting everyone know that the powers-that-be were once again trying to crimp the flow of knowledge. Other duties were less glamorous, but based on equally stern principles: keep the JPL open to all – and free of charge. Need I add that the largest part of JPL's clientele was scholars completing projects, or students on assignments with nowhere else to go, and still is? We wanted to ensure that they had the best.

It was an old British leftish thing about the democracy of wisdom, I suppose. And when I visited the New York Public Library recently I thought back to our square barrack with its three arches reaching up the steps to a suitable Latin inscription, its bold statues on every corner, blocking the end of the gardens at Market Square, and I mumbled to myself with a certain patriotic pride: *we did it first*. The greatness of every city's intellectual life depends on its library, after all.

Sometimes I remind myself that I sat on that committee with no less than Professor Raymond Dart. He was in his nineties then, resembling one of his palaeolithic skulls and still very Australian in his speech. He warned us how these expensive new computers were going to take over from the tradition of cheap books and how knowledge would become ever more inaccessible to the masses and he was right.

I wish I'd gone back to Herman Charles Bosman who, in 1931, met his future wife serving the browsers across the Reference Library desk. Striding back there in 1947, where else could he find copies of his own short stories to compile his *Mafeking Road*, but in the bound copies of *New Sjambok* and *The S.A. Opinion* filed in the stacks under Q. St. 364 and so on? I consult the same holdings; without them, of the work of our greatest South African writer of the twentieth century there would be no trace. Nor would most of the history of our city be preserved, for what most Johannesburgers do not know is that in the vaults – yes, in a floor of its own, right underneath the Harry Hofmeyr parking garage – are stored miles and miles of complete newspaper runs of

everything from day one of, say, *The Standard and Diggers'
News*. Those pages, friable and crackling now, may be con-
sulted by anyone with the curiosity and the patience. If you
are half a researcher, get your work clothes on and breathe
the authentic dust. And, no, nothing vaguely like that type of
information is available on the Internet.

I suppose the committee could have kept on functioning
indefinitely, exercising our principles and performing our duties
– keeping our city great – had not a few external factors inter-
vened. When I am asked by any contemporary councillor
presiding over the current demise of our city how much I was
paid to work on the Consultative Committee (always that is
the first question – and they want to know not just the hourly
rate, but the allowance for expenses, for transport and for
entertainment as well), I hum a bit and make the point that
voluntarily meant unpaid. We shuffled into the librarian's
parlour to endorse her procedures for the free tea and the
lemon cake, if you like. Chocolate cake for a bumper month.

In the 1990s the quality of that free fare began to deterio-
rate, however. Soon we were down from lemon sponge to
lemon creams, as the booklist shrank with rising prices. For
years on end we unwillingly had to cull periodical sub-
scriptions, advising each in our area on what would be least
missed in a world-class collection. Soon after 1994 it was
Marie Biscuits: budget cuts. The entire booklist was down
from an hour and a half's work to a few minutes.

The times of meetings had to be changed (staff were being
mugged if they went home late). And then we had to be taken
by friends (our cars were being stolen). Soon we had to phone
in first to ask if there were demonstrations blocking access.

There was a crisis with summer rains. The waste of the
squatter community in the sloping entrances had washed into
the stacks, where the air conditioning was coating the entire
Strange Collection in a urinous vapour. I shared their feelings
of dismay, saving Bosman underground, hanging on to the

overhead sparking electric trolleys to cross puddles of dead rats and human turds.

And then the library budget was cut altogether, to zero. At that moment JPL – now called the Greater Johannesburg Public Library – lost its contact with all the developing world, slid back into becoming history itself. For those who feel the opening of learning gets interesting precisely where IT expands, that is where Johannesburg closed itself off. The last minute of the Consultative Committee, as we voted ourselves out of existence in January 2001, was plain enough. The reason was Business: None.

So I have become an old codger in turn, after my eighteen years of free service at the JPL. I have been known to moan about the dirt clogging the fountain outside and the fact that all those valiant professional ladies, instead of medals, have had early pensions forced on them. Take it as read that I understand my city's greatness has moved elsewhere.

Stephen Gray was born in Cape Town in 1941 but has been based in Johannesburg since 1969, where he lives and works as a freelance writer near the central business district. He is a poet and novelist, and is currently editing the works of Herman Charles Bosman.

Nightmare in Northern
Suburbia

Anne Hammerstad

She knew something was wrong as soon as she made her usual left turn into the parking lot. There were parking spaces. Not one here and there, but all over the place, like gaping, frayed holes in the tapestry of suburban living. She took a deep breath. This was not the time for hyperventilation. She stepped on the gas and drove determinedly to the parking space just outside the main entrance, the one next to Woolworths. A thrill of excitement rippled down her spine. Never before in her many years in northern suburbia had she been able to park in this most coveted of parking spaces in this most popular of malls. She closed her eyes and took another deep breath. Something was wrong. Very wrong.

It was a Saturday afternoon, but with no bustle. Woolworths was open but empty. Five till ladies stared at her as she walked by, as if they knew something she didn't. She decided to do her usual routine, one perfected through aeons of Saturday shopping afternoons. Straight through the mall, down one level, to start the day's shopping at Pick'n'Pay. From there, leisurely but systematically weave through the crowds while staking out the clothes shops. The finishing post was always the same, and so was the reward: at the café adjoining Exclusive Books, she would sit down with a satisfied smile, coffee in one hand and the latest issue of *House and Garden* in the other. But today the lack of cushioning shopping bodies made the walls throw the sound of her clicking heels back at her with surprising aggression. Doggedly sticking to her routine, she could feel her feet slowing down. Dragging. Finally stopping. The unnaturally loud but regular sound of her breathing took over from the sound of her high-heeled shoes. A quick gasp escaped from the wrinkles of her pursed lips when she realised that the doors of her favourite café were firmly shut.

Standing nailed to the ground by the silence surrounding her, she could feel a rage she did not even know she had well up inside her. A throbbing, bursting, red sensation that could only be overcome through violence. Her gun was in the glove compartment of the car, but there wasn't anyone around who was particularly deserving of getting shot. In fact, there was nobody around. Only an eerie, empty atmosphere wearing down her nerves, and atmospheres only laugh at you if you try to shoot them.

If only there were some hijackers around, she thought. That would at least have been something tangible, something familiar, something you could point your gun at.

The throbbing subsided. She was not sure how long she had been standing outside the bolted doors of Exclusive Books, but the mall was as empty as when her rage attack had begun. Then she glimpsed from the corner of her eye a grey shadow hurrying along, following the contours of the wall. The shadow started when she spoke to it. Her voice sounded strange, too loud and too shrill in the unused air conditioned air. But it stopped to answer her nevertheless.

Where is everyone?

I don't know, I hardly ever come here. I hate the place, but had some errands that couldn't be postponed any longer.

Some student type, she gathered. Young, alternative, smug. The gun in her glove compartment loomed in her mind, but she managed to shake the image out of her head. Instead she aimed her stride at a wealthy-looking woman in her fifties who had appeared at the top of the escalator. The woman had a sad and tired air despite her plastic surgeons' efforts. She was easily recognisable as Mrs Kurtz, one of the Saturday shopping regulars.

Oh, you know, dear, I don't come here very often any more. My husband says I must get a more wholesome hobby than the mall. Something more in line with nation building.

Nation building? But Mrs Kurtz was off at a half-trot towards Exit Five without giving an explanation. A great sadness and fatigue of sympathy gripped her when she realised that a woman once admired by all as the backbone of Mall Culture had now plainly gone mad.

EHRM.

She turned around and looked straight at the bursting seams of a police officer's shirt. Further up was the knitted brow and moustachioed lip of the shirt's owner.

Loitering, are we?

Loitering?

Are you mocking me, Madam?

No, I just thought that malls were made for loitering?

MADAM, that may have been true in the unreconstructed days, but today every patriotic South African knows her duty is to avoid malls. Now, move on.

She scurried towards the exit, in the footsteps of Mrs Kurtz, a haze of confusion blocking her thoughts. Where to now? It was only 11 am, and she never started her rose pruning until after lunch. It was a matter of principle. Her mother had always said that a life without routines was a life empty, and today's collapse of schedule left her with the prospect of one and a half hours of emptiness. At least there was the option of aimless driving through the leafy avenues of Parkview, Parkwood, Parkhurst and the other Parks, she remembered with a sigh of relief. The freedom of the road always did wonders for her soul – as long as it was enjoyed in the safety of the neighbourhood, of course.

The police constable tapped on her car window. Apprehensively she rolled it down.

Where are you going, Madam?

Oh, driving . . .

I am sure you know the new law, then? Here is a leaflet, in case you need to be reminded.

He thrust the leaflet into her hand and marched off.

HIGHWAY CODE 2002

The new Highway Code for National Unity, taking effect from 2002-07-31:

1. Cars are a mode of transport of last resort and their use is illegal for distances less than two kilometres. Pensioners and other valid permit holders excluded.
2. When using a car, adhering to rule 1 above, the shortest route between departure and destination must be chosen.
3. Recreational and other forms of mindless driving is strictly forbidden, unless it is to the Apartheid Museum or Newtown Cultural Precinct.
4. Arrive alive.

Metropolitan Police

The truth hit her like a rock: post-apartheid is upon us, she gasped, and this time it was for real. One could only marvel that it had taken them that long to figure it out, she mused, letting out an involuntary giggle. Then she pulled herself together and drove home solemnly. Her anxiety and rage had given way to a quiet sort of relief.

Well, she thought, I could take up a Saturday course in Zulu, or maybe in Xhosa – I have always wanted to learn how to do those funny clicks. She took a right turn out of the parking lot and never looked back.

Anne Hammerstad is a journalist and academic living in Johannesburg. When she is not writing her DPhil thesis on refugee politics, she writes for Norway's Dagbladet.

Getting Even

Heidi Holland

I came home late one night to a near-death experience. A man appeared from nowhere, clamped his hands around my throat, thumb nails cutting into my skin, and hissed 'Don't scream', his face an inch from mine. Another person whose face I didn't see was holding a gun to my temple. The dog must have thought it was an embrace because I could see his tail wagging in my peripheral vision as I pirouetted on tiptoe, desperate to breathe. I thought I was within a gasp of being killed.

It is hard to comprehend what happens to you deep down after such an attack. It hurt my heart and muddled my thoughts for months. You don't get over it, I suspect, as much as learn to live around it. For a long time, perhaps forever, it creeps up behind you and pounces anew.

I worried that it would leave me so nervous that I wouldn't be able to live alone any more, so I put my house on the market. I often wondered if the horror in my eyes ever bothered my attacker in flashbacks, the way the indifference in his haunted me. I asked myself why a lot, even though I knew the answer.

I wondered if there were secret schools around Jo'burg where armed robbers learned how to locate the larynx in a flash and squeeze it rather than the surrounding muscle and connective tissue, as an amateur strangler might do. Or if there were crime consultants teaching psychological methods of preventing women from screaming, like apologising while frisking the victim in search of weapons so she'd know she wasn't going to be raped. Or dropping keys on the floor when you left her, bound and gagged, so she'd feel less helpless, less likely to scream.

These were bizarre thoughts based not only on the cold professionalism of my attackers but on a sociological revelation I had in Soweto several years ago while researching a book.

Pimville on a Wednesday evening at 5.30; the heat of the day hung oppressively in a small room tightly packed with young men and a few boys, fourteen of them, talking and yelling at each other and jostling as if in a shower room after a football match. A television set blared on a footstool wedged in a corner, swaying a bit from the vibrations of kicking legs.

The youths sprawled on to the floor, lounged on tatty chairs, sat in one another's laps. Two engaged in a wrestling contest, their bodies lurching against others who protested irritably. The room reeked with the smell of marijuana. A middle-aged woman appeared in the doorway, looking pained and making calming gestures with her hands, but they took no notice. As she retreated, the youths yelled for silence. Every eye was now trained on the television.

They were watching 'The Bold and the Beautiful', a Hollywood soap opera screened daily in South Africa. Typical of its genre, the show features immaculately groomed, exclusively white men and women engaged in various modes of hedonism and revenge in exotic locations. The Soweto youths were trans-fixed. On the screen was a blonde beauty lying in a cool white hospital bed, her eyes brimming with tears as she uttered dec-larations of love to her suave husband. The scene cut to another bed, this time containing the naked body of the same man romping with a different, equally lovely woman. The camera panned briefly around their stylish celluloid love nest, picking up symbols of wealth – a magnum of champagne in a giant silver ice bucket, an art treasure displayed on a marble plinth, jewels casually strewn over the dressing table. Then the action moved to a polished mahogany boardroom, where a silver-haired tycoon was plotting the demise of his business partner.

The half-hour programme seemed to end all too soon for the mesmerised youths. As the credits rolled on to the screen and the familiar signature tune played out, they sat in silence for a while. A leg stretched out to punch the television's trans-mission switch. Though the screen was blank, still they stared at it, reluctant to stir from the spell. Slowly, stretching cramped limbs, they began to rise and the din enveloped the room once more.

But the mood had changed. Sullenly, most of the youths filed out into the street, gathering in the fading light to plan the night's activities. Some – including an aggressive sixteen-year-old who was repeating phata-phata, meaning sex, in a monotonous, drugged tone – walked off to visit girlfriends. Some went home in hope of a meal. Others strolled to a nearby shebeen to drink. Three were left in the street, standing together, speaking in quiet voices for a long time. A few lingered in the room, still willing to talk to me as arranged.

It was dark now and the figures of the youths outside were shadowy in the dim light of a lone street lamp. They were planning ukuspina. 'It is when you go to steal,' explained a youth in the house who knew their plans. 'All of us do this when we need money. We steal cars, or from shops. Anywhere there is dulas we can take it. They will go to a white part of

Johannesburg when it is late. They can hire a car and also guns if they do not have them. These majita have guns. I myself have a gun. It is my helping hand.

'They will drive in the white man's streets, looking for a house or a car. They are thinking about 'The Bold and the Beautiful'; all that is going on in the beautiful houses where the whites have too much money, everything, and we black dogs have nothing. That is why we watch 'The Bold and the Beautiful'. It reminds us how much the whites have got. It gives us strength and courage to spin and maybe rape, ya man. Ek wil eet. I must steal to get money. I don't want to die from malnutrition. I'd rather die a hero, stealing a car, supporting my family. Hey, man, it's OK. If we have to start them, we will do it. We are not scared.'

While his friends were offering similar testimonies to justify violent crime, one of them passing out on the sofa mid-sentence, a nineteen-year-old with a prison record walked into the room peeling an orange with a long knife. Its sharpened blade gleamed menacingly as he halted beside me, much too close for normal discourse. 'Are you scared?' he asked. The others in the room howled with laughter as I admitted: 'Yes, I'm scared.'

Since that strange evening in Pimville, I've known what it's like to be terrified, never mind scared. But I've recovered, more or less, and stopped asking myself why. I've thought a lot over the years about what those youths told me, and I could go on contemplating the deep lines of alienation that scar Jo'burg society until I'm blue in the face. But I'd still have to scream: Hey, man, it's not OK.

Heidi Holland is a journalist and author of books on the liberation struggle, Soweto and Africa's traditional belief system. She is

tempted sometimes to use the pseudonym Primrose Tshabalala to avoid accusations of cultural colonialism that often come her way because whiteness is thought in some quarters to disqualify otherwise competent writers from sticking their noses into aspects of black culture.

Who? Me? A Racist?

Michael Holman

I am starting to miss apartheid. I can no longer get a room at the Mount Nelson, or a compartment on the Blue Train. Flights are full, and my dream of a cottage at Hermanus is receding as rapidly as prices are rising.

I stood in the immigration queue at Jan Smuts airport, cross and exhausted after a ten-hour flight, and reflected on these tribulations. But at the heart of my discontent was something more profound.

I was missing the tension of a township funeral. I recalled the electric atmosphere at the Johannesburg Market Theatre during the brutal decade of the 1980s. Just being part of the audience, watching a Barney Simon production about contemporary South Africa, seemed to be a political statement. But it was more than this. I missed the stress that bonded the friendships forged by adversity.

As I stood, the queue hardly moving, I realised that Nelson

Mandela's inauguration marked the day they shot my fox.

Apartheid was the issue which allowed moral certainty, the glorious conviction that right and wrong was black and white. These are now grey days in South Africa, thank goodness. The euphoria of the election has faded, and those certainties, those moral absolutes are harder to define.

In their place are admirable plans to build a million houses a year, or bring electricity to the townships. But 'Forward with the Reconstruction and Development Plan' does not have the same ring as 'Free Nelson Mandela'.

When apartheid was swept away, we journalists made the best of the good news. We exchanged anecdotes at The Ritz, the northern suburbs restaurant that served as an informal press club, its entrance guarded by a man with an Uzi, although his colleague preferred a sawn-off shotgun. To the secret regret of some of us, it was the closest we got to violence.

Nelson Mandela's inauguration was marked with a celebratory dinner and a poem written in honour of the occasion:

> O what joy to be a hack,
> As power shifts from white to black!
> O what bliss to be alive,
> When a British pound can buy rands five.

So I miss apartheid. Perhaps the immigration officer detected my malaise, as I stood in the queue at Jan Smuts. The queue was black, for most of the passengers had come off a flight from Angola. Only two desks were open at the immigration counter. A third was marked 'SA passport holders only'.

A white immigration officer stands, arms folded, in the hall, surveying the scene. I catch his eye, and thus a conversation begins. It is conducted in the sign language of mzungus in Africa, expressing their frustrations and impatience. Gone are the days when such irritations could be expressed aloud.

But through the silent changes of expressions, a lifted eyebrow here, a fleeting grimace there, a twitch of the shoulders, an upward glance to the heavens, we exchange views. I catch his eye. 'See?' his expression is saying. 'This is what happens. Let one in, and then they all want to come.'

I gave a discreet 'Bit of a nuisance this' gaze at the heavens.

His lips pursed a fraction. 'We've got to live with this . . . all right for you, you are just a visitor.'

But colour bonding was having its effect. A split second tilt of his chin in the direction of the SA passport holders' desk spoke volumes. 'Join the other queue,' the gesture said, 'it will be quicker.'

I dislike racists and queue jumpers with equal passion, but ten hours in economy class, sandwiched between fellow passengers with whom I had lost the battle of the arm rests, drained my patience and undermined my principles.

But I needed reassurance. I made a quick side to side glance as if to say 'Who, me?'

He maintained eye contact. 'Get a move on, before someone sees us.' I had hesitated too long. A terrible suspicion was growing in his mind. But for both of us, it was too late to turn back.

I had picked up my bag, avoiding eye contact with the patient travellers in front of me. My fractional hesitation, however, tells him volumes. Twenty yards now divides us, as I move to the shorter, adjoining queue, but his upper lip has a momentary sneer.

I look away.

'Aagh you liberals.' I almost hear a contemptuous rolling of the 'r', the more pronounced for having unwittingly assisted someone whom he thought might be sympathetic.

'Aagh you liberals. Full of talk.'

Michael Holman has written on and from Africa for the *Financial Times* since 1975. He lives in London. 'Who? Me? A racist?', written in 1995, first appeared in his book *African Deadlines*. Seven years on, a British pound can buy around rands fifteen.

Jo'burg Blues

Christopher Hope

Flying in, eye to eye with the winking pools, the smudge on the horizon that is the city. Jo'burg, Joeys, Jewburg, Jozi . . . a place my mother called 'town'. When I was growing up, we took the tram to town, and men in Jeppe Street wore hats, and women sipped tea in Ansteys, wearing white gloves. Paul Kruger called the place Sodom and Gomorrah and everyone who didn't live there thought he was putting it mildly. They still do. From the dusty sprawl in the southwest that is Soweto, to the swanking suburbs heading forever north, the pursuit of wealth is inversely proportionate to the loss of cerebral matter.

On the airport road into town two BMW convertibles neck and neck, hoods down, came barrelling past and I swear one driver had a cellphone in his ear. The Jo'burg earring. The boys were having fun. Dark and often fatal fun. Jo'burg fun. The word is 'dicing'. It catches that curious blend of cockiness, aggression and fatalism one might call Jo'burg noir. So you get wiped out on the motorway – or playing the slots. But if you're going to go – may as well stay in the fast lane. It's all dicing, anyway. Isn't it, hey? So fuck you – arsehole! Suck my exhaust.

Welcome to Jo'burg – have a nice day.

On the side of the airport road is the familiar, fearsome clutter. Some child-giant got tired of his toys and has thrown them out of his cot. Low-browed office parks, pompous warehouses, and a clenched fist of houses sphincter-tight behind beautiful walls, Jo'burg's trademark, the anal-retentive suburb. And then the brand new architecture of liberation – the Romano-kitsch casino, a thousand slot machines wrapped around a shopping mall.

But then what do you expect? This is a town that thought mine dumps were pretty, that had a soft spot for slimes dams, and thanked God he had given it a reef of gold beneath its feet. The mine dumps are shrinking. Years ago they hung around town like drunks on day release from the detox clinic. The sandy equivalents of meths drinkers in Joubert Park. Scrubby grass like fierce unshaven stubble grew over their yellow faces. Thing was – you liked them, you blushed a bit when visitors said 'what do you do with them?'

Some bright spark took one of these sandcastles, sheered off its head and planted a drive-in movie on the crest. Great stuff. Someone had an even better idea. What about tearing down the dumps and taking them to the cleaners all over again, for the pinpoints of gold they didn't give up first time round?

Very Jo'burg.

I dropped down the off-ramp into a place called Motor-town, into the grid of streets adorned with the names of this city's singular rip-off merchants, its energetic scoundrels, its gold-diggers who built a brothel and a bourse, and never could tell the difference. Not then, not now, not ever – Loveday,

Harrison, Rissik and Jeppe . . . Once-upon-a-time Jo'burg preserved in the poetry of their names.

The headlines roped to the lamp-posts sing the old dark songs – golden city blues –

Ten Shot Dead in Bed

Pregnant Housewife's Poisoned Present

School Hall Stolen

Here is the Carlton Centre. To build it they had to excavate a hole, and not just any hole, the hole was the biggest, best urban hole anywhere in Africa. Nowhere in the southern hemisphere was there a hole to touch it – and people came from all over the place just to look at the hole. No one anywhere, said the people of Jo'burg, dug better holes or dug them faster, or deeper, or sunk more money into them. The Carlton hole was big enough to swallow the Empire State Building (if melted down). It did no good wondering aloud how you'd melt down the Empire State. Or why? The Carlton sneered at such questions; fifteen acres of hole was going to contain shops, restaurants, pavement cafés, movie houses and an ice-rink. On top of the hole was the tower – it was going to be fifty storeys high, it was going to be the tallest tower in Africa. And next to the tower, its rich twin would be the best luxury hotel in creation. And on top of the tower there would be an observation room that would allow you to look thirty miles into the distance. On a really clear day you might see as far as Pretoria.

The accomplices of the mining house tycoons were the New York architects Skidmore, Owings and Merrill, who seemed to have risen to the challenge of designing – even by the record standards of the 1960s – one of the most brutally ugly buildings on the planet. And how we loved it! We had the deepest hole, tallest tower, richest hotel in the country – it was very, very Jo'burg. Soon we were talking in awe of its room prices, its silver cutlery. Its sheer hulking brutal Jo'burg pizzazz, its gold-plated nerve. And the skating was fine.

We boasted about the Carlton – it was said to be the greatest concrete erection in the world – another triumph attributed to those razzle-dazzle boys who ran the town. Their collective names were spoken in that peculiar reverent drawl that is Jo'burg at prayer, whenever money, gold, big bucks, moolah is mentioned – creators of all that was good and profitable, they turned bare veld into bullion, the Godlings of Hollard Street who were collectively worshipped as the Mahninghowzez . . . See how the knee bends, the head bows at the magical invocation of true, ingot-dripping, bullion-loaded dazzle. And why not? Since buying shares or salting a gold mine is as close as most Jo'burgers ever came to a truly religious experience.

Oh boy, oh boy, oh boy. I drive past the hulking wreck of the Carlton, Jo'burg's own Titanic. All that energy, that wealth, that colour, all sunk. The hotel boarded up, the silver cutlery flogged, the ice-rink melted, even the guards who used to accompany hotel guests on shopping trips have been sacked. And the Carlton, like central Jo'burg, is a place where no one walks, a crumbling eerie ramshackle wreck. By day the office workers scurry through their tunnels to their offices, and flee come sunset. At night it is muggers, the homeless, the hijackers who seethe around the deserted tower.

Jo'burg, my town, slipped north, leaked, left, ran out, dribbled away, leaving the Carlton standing in a shell-shocked skyline. I went up on top of the Carlton recently, Jimmy from Soweto was there and he thought I'd been too long away to watch my back alone. 'I'll cover for you when you use the ATM,' said Jimmy, 'no one from Soweto shops here . . . folks in their right minds don't come here.'

I know what he means. I think I might drive through the

streets after dark with a bullhorn calling: 'Anybody there?' – and get no answers. Sometimes, after dark, downtown, you feel Jo'burg's been hit by a neutron bomb that killed all the people but it left the skyline standing.

I want to go skating at the Carlton again. I want to walk down Harrison and Fox and Commissioner, I want to feel the old heart – built, it must be said, of solid brass and damn cheek – beating again. If Jo'burg doesn't jive then nowhere does. I know it is an invented city, I know it talks big in its names, I know there are no Saxons in Saxonwold, no Forests in Forest Town, no monarch in Sandringham – no one called Bez ever lived in Bez Valley, and you never could see the park from Parkview. So what? Jo'burg is the single metropolis in southern Africa worthy of the name, the greatest city south of Cairo, it has more energy in its smallest, furthest, tiny fingertip of a suburb than entire other cities. Cape Town is a cute little place with a hill in the middle of town – Durban is a doze on the beach. Nothing could be worse than the rumour that Jo'burg has been hijacked by merchant bankers and kugels, and was last seen heading north, in the back of a Porsche.

Christopher Hope was born in Johannesburg and now lives in France. His first work of non-fiction, *Separate Development*, was banned in South Africa shortly before he went into exile. He has written seven novels, including *Serenity House* which was short-listed for the Booker Prize in 1992. His latest novel, *Heaven Forbid*, is set in Johannesburg.

Hiding from the truth

Jonah Hull

I have a confession to make. It's a secret I have held darkly for some years now, though I thought little of it at the time. I voted for the Soccer Party in South Africa's first democratic election.

In April 1994, millions queued for days in the dusty late summer sun to cast a vote for freedom. If anything was assured during that turbulent time, it was that the majority would win, the people's voice would finally be heard. Where was I on that momentous occasion? Standing on the sidelines is the answer, in the face of the triumphant juggernaut of people's power as it lurched unstoppably towards the very heart of Afrikaner pride, ethnic purity and decades-long dominance. I voted neither openly and proudly for the rampant ANC, nor secretively for the Nats, as I know many of my friends did while proclaiming their wholehearted enthusiasm for the impending about-face of power.

I cast my X next to a face I didn't recognise, a name I'd never heard before. A white pseudo-hippy whose cause was hardly political. I don't recall the party credo too clearly, but a line about legalising cannabis rings a bell. I did it because they offered to buy two thousand of my T-shirts, duly embossed with their logo of a soccer ball. The shirts were cheap two-rand jobs a friend and I had thrown together with a clever motif showing a hand raised in a victory salute, the index and third finger forming a V with 'OTE' inscribed next to it. A week before the vote, we'd sold only a handful. Hours spent at a variety of flea markets around Johannesburg had produced little more than snarled insults, guffaws and much gesturing of hands showing us the V-sign the other way round. Then the Soccer Party happened along. Our money for your vote, they offered. It seemed fair enough. No, it was irresistible. The question is: how could I have been so apathetic?

As with most questions that inspire a little soul-searching, it raises a larger one; one which most of my generation of white South Africans have come to ask themselves quietly at some point. How did we carry on through our teens and early twenties – the traditional years of human revolution – so unshaken by the fires burning in townships on our doorstep, by racial and ethnic hatred, abuse, violence and murder? Wasn't it the students of Soweto who first lit those fires in 1976? And weren't some of our predecessors at Wits University shot at, beaten and arrested by police during the 1980s protest marches down Yale Road? Didn't occasional protests by black students in Senate House descend into violent standoffs with police and snarling dogs, disrupting our lunch hour? Why were we not more moved, by conscience if nothing else? The answer has to do with a sickness that plagues white South Africans. It's called hiding from the truth, and most of us suffer from it still.

I spent long hours during those days and nights in a lively, bohemian bistro called, appropriately enough, the Question

Mark. Located in Jo'burg's trendiest suburb, Melville, you could eat cheaply there and drink until dawn. In the year or so before the elections, the Question Mark was a testing ground for the new attitudes and ideas creeping into people's lives. The press hung out there, foreign and local, as did a motley band of musicians, actors, students and academics. While there were never many blacks around apart from the kitchen staff, it was a place where, theoretically, all races were welcome. I liked to think that was the case anyway.

We had no real black friends with whom to test the theories, and 'integration' was a word that found little context in our conversations. Nevertheless, over ice buckets full of Black Labels we argued both sides of the divide: why it was right that the ANC win the election, who was going to vote for them and who wasn't in favour of a strong opposition as the cornerstone of an effective democracy. All fuelled by our sudden and fashionable outrage now that apartheid and the Nats were so exposed. For months we sat at the same tables, talking the same shit, never a black face in sight. Who were we kidding? Only ourselves, the better to go home feeling we were somehow 'engaged with the process'. It wouldn't have gone down well at all to have mentioned that I'd voted for the Soccer Party.

It was said after Nelson Mandela's release from Pollsmoor Prison in 1990 that it was hard to find a white South African who'd ever supported apartheid. We closed ranks on the truth and scrambled for a moral high ground that put as much distance as possible between us and the past. We were all complicit, but my generation especially because we had the least to lose. As passionate young adults, with all the opportunity in the world, we should have seen the writing on the wall and stood up for it. Not when we had to look good, but when we were struck by it in our hearts. Then it would have mattered. But few of us did. What awful conclusion are we to draw from that?

I suggest, as thoroughbred white South Africans, we have racism in our bones. I've wanted to interrupt many a politically polished Jo'burg dinner party, then watch the sanctimonious choke on mouthfuls of roast beef and fine Cape Shiraz: 'I am a racist, and YOU are a racist!' Haven't we all developed deep instincts over time that cause us to rail against the opposite race? No matter how we present outwardly, don't whites privately believe they're superior to blacks?

The subject is taboo, and I will doubtless be damned for raising it publicly like this. However, no amount of political correctness should prohibit us from real self-examination. It's the only way towards a society based on freedom and equality. We should ask ourselves and each other, at our informed, intelligent, middle-class soirées, whether we really are the family of smiley, happy black and white faces we project to the world. Lean over and whisper the question to the black person sitting opposite. There isn't one? Huh!

What we're creating is a society based upon hypocrisy and dishonesty. There is no freedom to express the inequality we feel. That whites and blacks are inherently suspicious of each other, that we all have deeply held convictions about the ethics, morality and integrity of the other, are things that need to be laid bare if we're to achieve genuine harmony between the races. We need to 'fess up, come clean, say it like it is. If this is the ghastly truth, no wonder we choose to hide from it.

Jonah Hull is a producer and cameraman for the television news arm of the Associated Press, APTN. He is currently based in Geneva, and misses Johannesburg every day he's away.

Soweto Trip

Nicole Itano

The famous township of Soweto is a vast, sprawling maze of streets for which there are no maps and few street signs. Directions are often given by landmarks: left at the Castle Beer sign, right past the little clearing with the pile of trash. Since I inevitably miss these local landmarks and end up desperately lost, I usually go there with a guide.

Not long after I moved to South Africa, however, I ventured there alone to interview pensioners who, because of Aids and unemployment, were now supporting their children and grandchildren on their tiny monthly government payments. For once, I knew where I was going, although months later I learned that to follow the one path I knew into Soweto, I had driven halfway around the city, a not inconsequential distance in a place that sprawls on for miles. With my interviews finished, I headed back home in my battered, sky-blue Mazda. I was almost back to the main road and congratulating myself on my navigational skills, when a policeman waved me over.

Panic hit me. What had I done wrong? Was I speeding? Were my registration papers in order? Had I forgotten to use my turn signal? I had not yet realised that in South Africa random roadblocks were perfectly legal and that the police had every right to search my car at whim.

I turned off my engine, rolled down the window and waited, hands on the steering wheel as I had been taught in driver's education in the United States years before. The policeman, a portly, middle-aged black man, came to my window and looked in.

'What's a nice white girl like you doing in Soweto?' he said, the disapproval in his voice indicating his belief that nice white people don't go wandering around in Soweto.

He's largely right. Most white South Africans have never been to Soweto or any of the other townships where most urban black South Africans still live. On the plane ride to Johannesburg, I had sat next to a white university student from Pretoria who had even warned me against going into the central business district. 'It's too dangerous,' he said, hinting, but not saying, that there were too many black people there these days.

Still, I was somewhat shocked by the policeman's comment. No one had ever called *me* white before. Asian, Latino, Hawaiian, Native American, Turkish and just about everything else under the sun, but never white.

'I'm not white,' I blurted out, launching automatically into the abbreviated ethnic history I have developed to answer the inevitable question, 'Where are you from, anyway?'

He looked at me strangely, as if not quite sure what to do with this tiny American woman who was spurting off a list of countries where her ancestors had come from: Japan, Mexico, a Sioux Indian reservation, Ireland. That wasn't really the answer he was looking for. Finally, he coughed and said, 'Well, here you're white.' An uncertain pause, and then: 'Licence and registration?'

As I riffled through my glove compartment to retrieve my brand new registration and international driver's licence, I realised that here in South Africa I was on the other side of the race divide. In America, I was an ethnic minority and my perceptions about race were coloured by the experiences of my family who had been interned during World War Two, denied jobs and education and forbidden to marry outside their ethnic group.

But as far as the policeman was concerned, in South Africa I was part of the privileged elite. I was a foreigner with enough money to move halfway around the world, driving my own car (albeit an old and clunky one) back to my comfortable, security-enhanced apartment in the suburbs. As I sat there in my car waiting to hear my fate from the policeman, I realised that he was right.

Johannesburg is a fairly cosmopolitan place and Melville, the trendy suburb where I live, is one of the city's more integrated neighbourhoods, filled with professionals with all shades of skin and timbres of accent. There certainly isn't complete racial equality – a disproportionate number of whites still fill the tables at expensive restaurants and blacks continue to occupy the lowest tier of jobs as dishwashers, street hawkers and car guards – but there you could pretend for a while that this was not a country still deeply tormented by its past.

But Melville, and the handful of other places like it in Johannesburg, are oases in a country still largely segregated by race. While they were getting slowly darker, thanks to the migration of newly empowered blacks, coloureds and Indians, areas like Soweto were still almost entirely homogeneous. There were certainly no whites moving to Orlando or Mandela Park, and I, with my light skin and American accent, stuck out like a sore thumb in Soweto. On another trip to Soweto, months later, I was relieved of my handbag at a gas station while enquiring for directions (that time I had overestimated my directional ability). I suppose it was crystal clear to the robber that I wasn't from around those parts.

While I was lost in my own thoughts, the policeman examined my international driver's licence, a several-page long, yellow document, with confusion. 'See, it says right here that I can drive in South Africa,' I explained, pointing to the list of countries where the licence is valid. He sighed, handed it back to me and asked to look in the trunk of my car. After a cursory glance, he indicated that I could close the trunk and continue on my way. This time, it was my turn to be confused.

'That's it?' I asked. 'You're not going to give me a ticket?'

Nicole Itano moved to Johannesburg in 2001 to work as a free-lance reporter. She currently writes for The Christian Science Monitor and the Sydney Morning Herald and loves living in South Africa. She grew up in the mountains of Colorado.

In celebration of walls

Frank Lewinberg

Johannesburg is a city of walls. Walls surround virtually all homes and many of the city's major buildings. Walls clearly delineate private space from public space. They simultaneously define where those with the legitimate right of access may go, while excluding everyone else, denying them a formal entryway. Ironically, today Johannesburg's walls stand as a unique physical symbol of the dramatic changes that have swept through South Africa in the past twenty years.

It was not always so. Johannesburg was once a city with few walls, not unlike most European and North American cities. Low walls or planted hedges often served to separate the private from the public, establishing property limits but at the same time inviting the eye, conversation and even some limited access into the semi-private space that separates the public street from the private building within.

I grew up during the 1950s and 1960s in a middle-class

suburb of Johannesburg. As a white child, my neighbourhood felt safe, easy and comfortable. From a very young age, on foot or on my bike, I visited friends or went to the store. As a teenager, my friends and I continued to walk comfortably across the northern suburbs of Johannesburg day or night. We felt at ease and comfortable, and above all, both we and our parents felt safe. That was the apartheid city.

While there were no walls around our homes, we had an invisible wall around our lives, indeed around that massive area comprising the northern suburbs. We felt safe because the black people were not allowed to be there at night, certainly not after the set hour. We felt safe because the streets were continuously patrolled. We felt safe because we lived in an exclusive island of unreality. The walls were provided by the apartheid state, invisible to us white kids, but clearly visible to the eyes of black people. As a child I had no idea, no understanding, that the pattern of my daily life was circumscribed by such flimsy and differing perceptions, such double vision.

As apartheid began to crumble, the cocoon of the northern suburbs began to crumble with it. The police state was cracking to the tune of the children of Soweto. The police were being kept very busy in other places, and the safety and security of the northern suburbs was less easily assured. So white people took matters into their own hands and, house by house, the walls started to go up. It was no longer possible to guarantee safety at the expense of the state. What appeared to be a slow incremental process, in fact happened very quickly, in less than fifteen years. Today these walls have become a signature of Johannesburg.

To those from North America and Europe this looks like a step backwards. Should not the streets in neighbourhoods be inherently safe? Should not small children be able to play safely in public places? But the new Johannesburg is much more recognisable in many of the world's cities where there is a massive disparity in income levels across the society. The walls of Johannesburg are not unlike those emerging in Mexico City or São Paulo. It was apartheid that made Johannesburg feel like a North American or European city, a place from which the white folk had come. Now Johannesburg is not unlike its Latin American sisters. The reality of poverty, a small population of very affluent people living in a large population of very poor people, and a drastic shortage of jobs, these together shape the city.

In the immediate future, the removal of those walls is unlikely, an unrealistic and utopian vision. There are many problems to confront and safety and security are relatively small ones. It will ultimately be critical to address the issue of how to make the streets of Johannesburg safe, attractive and inviting again, but this will happen naturally if South Africans are able to address many of the more fundamental issues that they are today grappling with.

But for now we need to make the best of what we have. Indeed, Jo'burgers are a creative lot and as one travels across the city one notices a fine array of interesting new designs for walls. Pompous walls, ugly walls, walls of lush foliage and walls that have become wonderful entry gates. Transparent walls are made like historic ones, not unlike those surrounding many of the great buildings in Europe or even the White House. Slowly, Jo'burgers are beginning to find ways to integrate these walls, to make these walls less offensive.

Today Johannesburg is truly a post-apartheid city. Its walls are a signal of change in South Africa and a sign of a healthy and real city. Safety is no longer provided by the state at taxpayers' expense. It is provided by private owners of any racial group who need to buy their own security as they see it, and as such, security has been appropriately privatised. Let us celebrate the walls of Johannesburg as a signal of the fundamental change in the society, writ large along its streets, sweeping across its neighbourhoods. The walls of Johannesburg are a symbol that has become a part of the city's personality, and a fundamental part of the design and creation of Johannesburg today as it evolves.

Frank Lewinberg is an architect trained at Wits University. He is a city planner and has worked on assignments in Canada, the USA, Europe and the Caribbean.

Beyond our urban mishaps

Alan Lipman

If it's authentic local architecture you're after, you won't find it in the middle-class suburbs of Johannesburg. They are awash with impoverished mishaps, with crass imitations of elsewhere – anywhere but here. Travel instead to the immediate surroundings of our misshapen urban areas. That's where I went on returning from three decades in Europe. What follows is extracted from my notes of that memorable homecoming.

Architecture has long been the privilege of the privileged. Many millions of shack dwellers in Africa rely on their own resources and on their own design skills. These are considerable, particularly because they are rooted in first-hand knowledge of the daily needs of the dwellers. Driven by this thought, I visited some informal settlements – sometimes described as 'chaotic squatter camps' – in and around Johannesburg.

Far from formless, they are deliberately positioned shacks linked by major and lesser paths, some wide enough to be termed roads. They lead to spaza shops, communal water outlets, exits and entrances to the settlements, community assembly points of one sort or another.

Although crowded into small areas, the shacks do not intrude on neighbours. There is space around them for neighbourhood activities like trading with hawkers, watching casually over children at play, maintaining informal surveillance of the area, exchanging opinions with people from diverse backgrounds. There is space for many of the congenial attributes, the liveability factor, of urban – as against suburban – life which planning commentators like Jane Jacobs have ascribed to the local residential areas of cities like downtown New York, Rio de Janeiro, Bangkok and Paris.

These informal and effective arrangements are matched by similar, seldom officially recorded, social compacts. An example occurred recently when a colleague and I visited a section of Orange Farm – today one of Jo'burg's sprawling, so-called higgledy-piggledy squatter settlements – shortly after it had been established. Civil turmoil was, at that time, held to be endemic to sites of this nature.

Arriving at the outskirts of the settlement, we were approached by four young men who enquired about the purpose of our visit. My friend explained that he had come to show me the circumstances in which self-built shelters were being erected and occupied. The young men offered to assist us, first by indicating where his car might be parked in safety and shade. Then, while one of the group remained with the vehicle, the others guided us around the settlement, introducing us to some of the residents. Householders were invited to tell us why, how and when they had come to Orange Farm, to clarify the site layout for us and to indicate how they had constructed and were now using their homes.

We soon realised there was a shared understanding of how

life on the settlement could be conducted in an orderly, mutually satisfactory manner. We learned that the physical and social arrangements are not fortuitous: they are communally negotiated, endorsed by informal peer pressure and often by a written code of conduct. As key aspects of public life, they are appropriately, if not conventionally, civic.

In the arena of private life, most shanty-homes are maintained in a similarly ordered fashion, despite persistently adverse conditions. They are characterised by regularly swept earth forecourts, serried rows of neat washing-lines and all the other signs of attentive housekeeping that are visible to passers-by, even from vehicles speeding past on adjoining highways.

They are havens in a world of unmanaged urbanisation, seemingly entrenched unemployment, racial tensions, poverty and the lofty indifference with which 'respectable' society views the privations of 'squatter' life.

Most of the shacks I have visited are constructed of corrugated or sheet iron, plywood boarding and plastic sheeting. These adaptable, portable materials are fixed to metal or timber frames. A few dwellings stand on concrete surface beds, but the majority are not founded solidly. Roofs are sloped slightly to discharge rainwater and are held down by rocks. Unlike the picturesque adobe and thatch homes many shanty dwellers occupied before coming to Egoli, these are built from industrial products that have been assembled by people whose rapid adjustment to urban life is reflected in the structures.

As in all meaningful design, their houses link pragmatic and aesthetic issues. An example is the dual use of standard 'up-and-over' garage doors serving as an external wall at night or during poor weather and, in sunny conditions, as the tidily tucked away fourth side of an open veranda.

There are many other examples, from the quilt-art curtains providing privacy to the wondrously contrived shelving and ad hoc containers for storing clothes and other domestic items. And ingenious methods of space management of house-hold activities such as washing, ironing, cooking, sleeping and school homework.

Whatever else shack settlements lack – and that's a great deal – they are not without creative planning and design talent.

Alan Lipman practised as an architect in South Africa before he went into exile in 1963. He taught architecture at the University of Wales before returning to Johannesburg, where he has written on architecture for local publications. He writes a weekly newspaper column.

Old Eds

Barbara Ludman

The parking lot at the Old Eds gym in Houghton has got to be the classiest in Johannesburg. At peak times – say, 5.30 on a weekday afternoon – there are enough 4x4s to populate Maun, although the plethora of Pajeros and Land Rovers could use a splash of designer mud. The abundance of seven series BMWs, Mercs and Audi A6s would put the Saxon hotel's parking areas to shame. This wonderful informal motor show is watched over benignly by a couple of security guards dressed like French gendarmes sans capes, a nice touch considering the burgeoning population at Old Eds of Renaults and Peugeots.

Back when this Virgin Active flagship was the jewel in the crown of Leisurenet's Health and Racquet group, Old Eds was referred to by its substantial gay membership as the 'wealth and faggot'. But wealth isn't all Old Eds is about. For the past ten or twelve years, the club has been reflecting changes in the country, and it does that very well.

In the 1980s, it attracted a largely white clientele – not surprising, considering its location in a traditionally expensive white suburb. Then came 1990, the unbanning of liberation movements, the release of Nelson Mandela, the return, eventually, of exiles from London and Lusaka and Dar es Salaam, and the loosening of apartheid, which had been declared officially dead but unfortunately had gone on breathing.

The politicians found the gym first. In the early 1990s you could find yourself gasping and sweating on a stationary bicycle next to a future cabinet minister or a trade union leader on his way to a parliamentary list. It happened often: one journalist recalls walking into the men's sauna and interrupting a meeting between Anglo American's Michael Spicer, South African Communist Party leader Joe Slovo, and the National Union of Mineworkers' Marcel Golding, all wrapped about with towels, lacking only cigars. Black strugglistas were followed by black yuppies, or buppies – in many cases, one morphed into the other.

In its heyday, an estimated four thousand people worked out at Old Eds every day. It was a fashion-and-beauty show par excellence – the most fabulous bodies, male and female, encased in the most expensive leotards. The bodybuilders and the boxers added a bit of gravitas, and the school swimming teams a fair amount of noise. The thirty- and forty-something lawyers and academics trying to delay the inevitable made up a significant portion of the clientele, but there were also elderly women facing down osteoporosis with a determined assault on the circuit and old men taking a bit of gentle exercise. It was a cosmopolitan city on its own – all races, all ages, all shapes and sizes, although, of course, not all economic groups.

Then Leisurenet liquidated, with fraud charges laid against its joint CEOs, and Richard Branson volunteered to save the eighty-odd clubs. Branson said former president Nelson Mandela, who lives nearby, had asked him to save jobs by keeping the group going. It could be true; the helicopter that ferries Madiba around the country often uses Old Eds' playing fields as a landing pad, to the delight of those lucky enough to be around when it happens. When Branson's Virgin Active took over the group, it lost many of its members countrywide by the simple device of hiking its annual fees.

Did this affect Old Eds? Absolutely: one can get parking these days, even on a weekday evening. Many, angered by the fee rise, emigrated to greener pastures: the small, private gyms that flourished in the wake of the Leisurenet crash. But although other clubs may be suffering, many of Old Eds' regulars have come back, restoring what its manager refers to as a 'beautiful balance'.

They find much to contend with. As in the city itself, there's a continual attempt to 'upgrade', which means you're generally working out among flying dust and peeling carpet tiles. It's crowded with so many new machines in such a small space you've got to watch your elbows lest you wind up knocking out the guy thirty seconds ahead of you on the circuit. The redesign features flash colours, neon and Virgin rebranding, plus a truly awful layout; the old, cosy feel of the place has been diminished as the designers try to bunch like with like. Treadmills, bikes and similar machines are lined up in a 'cardio area' at the entrance, for example, battery hen style, facing television sets and fitted with a box that takes earphones.

If you bring your own you can plug them in, and you needn't engage with anybody. Presumably you're at the gym to work, not chatter and sightsee – a tough call for a place like Old Eds where schmoozing is part of the experience.

In any case there is less to gawk at these days, unless you go looking for it. The bodybuilders, who used to train in full public view next to the entrance, have been banished to the back, and the lunatics who spin now have their own space next to the changing rooms, out of the way.

One might wonder then why, with all the options on offer

– home gyms, small private gyms, other Virgin Active branches – people come back. Other clubs may be newer, bigger, glitzier; they may be better run. But there is a certain Jo'burg brashness that has not only survived but thrived since the takeover; a deal-making atmosphere; a lack of interest in race but a keen interest in status that suits people in this city. After all, if you're going to be run down by a bodybuilder on steroids, it may as well be a guy in a Porsche.

Barbara Ludman, for many years associate editor at the *Mail & Guardian*, is the author of several youth novels, including the award-winning *The Day of the Kugel*, and is co-editor of the A-Z *of South African Politics*.

Tatty whore with a heart of gold

Bongani Madondo

It's a freezing Wednesday morning when I get out of a taxi – one of those rickety jalopies promising to break apart while dashing around Johannesburg streets in a scary mix of speed, mayhem and fear. Out of the corner of my eyes in Bree Street struts a woman, sweet chocolate-skinned, horse-shaped face as stunning as that of ex-model and actor Dudu Mkhize. She comes straight towards me. Or in my direction, lest I flatter myself. I steal a closer look at her, almost as close as the dentist gets to the patient. Aaghh, as Rastafarians say, the sistah is indeed a queen of Sheba. A 'crea-shaun' of limitless beauty.

But as I look at the surroundings that woman is walking through, my jubilation shrinks to humiliation. I feel a stabbing pain thrust down my upper torso like Brutus finishing off Caesar. I have ventured into the inner city. As a black person and a resident of Johannesburg, my heart weeps as I look at tattered, old, smoky-smelling Jo'burg. Just for a moment that woman makes me forget about this decaying place. But as soon as she walks past this daily nagging reality returns: the rot and dirt, the spilling sewage, drug-infested needles, piles of vegetables and fruit composting on street corners.

I am lying. Something long ago died inside me about Johannesburg. I remember that when I was a hopeless literature student at a 'bush' varsity only one thing inspired me to go to English lectures. It was Nathaniel Nakasa's tour de force feature, 'Johannesburg, Johannesburg', published in a book *The World of Nat Nakasa*. Young and incurably impressionable as I was, the story brought a flush of pride. I had always loved Johannesburg. But Nakasa's use of imagery cemented my love for dear Johannesburg. Even when Mama Miriam Makeba sang the spirit-tormenting lament 'Gauteng, Gauteng, banna ba rona ba shwetse komponeng' (Jo'burg, Jo'burg, our husbands died in hostel compounds), I swore never to swerve from my love of Jo'burg.

It is Wednesday and I am taking an across-the-city stroll in a city I used to love. That Von Wielligh corner shop to which I travelled for more than a hundred kilometres while a teenager to buy a swanky Fifties-type Humphrey Bogart shirt is no longer there. Instead there is only a fried chicken outlet. Johannesburg is heaving with fried chicken everywhere. Upmarket, street gizzards, you name them, it's deep chickenland.

The subterranean citizens of the seedier parts of town on the eastern wing of Doornfontein mostly take over their territory when night falls. Down on the west wing of the business district, Diagonal Street is still civil to street traders, and Indian curry shops add a touch of glorious old Jo'burg. As a visitor here you have to be ready for a battle for your senses – between the blazing chillis and cinnamon from the Asian corner café and the vusa nduku herb shop next to it.

As you thrust further east along Bree Street, you soon

realise that the countdown to 8.30 pm at a nightclub that used to host the very best and smartest elites, Club Countdown – now called kwa Bangani – has already begun. It's getting late, and you can see the wobbly, boozy silhouettes of dangerous young men with fish-tail haircuts milling around. A big girl, barely dressed, passes by. There is a riot of whistles.

I stroll across Jozi as far as my old haunt, Mai Mai, the traditional market down in Jeppe where I used to savour the delicacies of tshisa nyama and chakalaka. It's no longer the same. It lacks the over-abundance of pre-94 colour and brandishing of 'traditional weapons' by Zulu hostel dwellers. As for the inner city itself, its dirt defeats tolerance. Ask me today whether I still love Johannesburg. How can anybody love such a barbarically dirty city?

Look around the Jozi landscape, if your eyes can sieve through the Himalayas of dirt and grime permanently layered on the city's streets, balconies and just anywhere. Go atop Ponte City or up the Hillbrow tower. Stretch your neck giraffe-like towards northern suburbia. What do you see? Spanking-clean suburbs. Protected and cleaned. Fresh air might even caress your nostrils there in suburbia. This is the story of many cities in one. I disagree with my renaissance-drunk friends that Johannesburg's infectious dirt and grime make it the truly African city that it ought to have been long ago. Unlike, they say with patriotic fervour, Cape Town, a piece of colonial Europe permanently plastered over the bottom of the dark continent.

A visitor touring Johannesburg and the adjoining suburban troika of hell, Judith's Paarl, Yeoville and Hillbrow-Berea, will think we are living in different cities to those far northern or eastern burbs. A new health hazard warning: beware dirt, general chaos, deteriorating buildings, paint peeling from the walls and dysfunctional drains. You'd swear it has been shelled by inner-city guerrilla warlords, like Maputo or Luanda. Every Tom, Dick and Skwiza buys a packet of fruit down at Ma Mlambo's stall near Park Station. They fill the stomach and dump the banana peels all over the pavement. A kaleidoscope of plastic and rubbish papers lies strewn across the streets. The bones of the Chicken Licken are already on the streets.

At the intersection of Twist and Plein, a passenger leans out the window of a taxi and – boom! – throws out a can of Coke. In the back alleys your nostrils are attacked by an overdose of flu from the yellowish, sepia-toned walls heavy with the aroma of informally brewed whiskey: takunyisa-soaked urine. Excuse me, am I soiling your Friday breakfast with this? Sorry.

At the front of those shops a young man with greenish teeth and Bangladeshi accent battles with a jumble-sale gogo from the townships for a place on the pavement. Music booms at a million decibels from a corner music bar. It's Brenda Fassie singing that she is not a weekend special any more. A BMW tears past at bullet speed, traffic cops hot on its tail. Two minutes after being stopped, its driver swaggers away from the cops in a hip'n'bounce pantsula attitude, grinning wildly.

Three girls with over-made-up faces and hairstyles your mama warned you about are still in the car. They beam at their BMW driver: 'How much?' The pantsula bloke, with a whole Carletonville gold mine on his neck – moqwebo honey – responds dismissively: Twenty rand. 'Is that all?' ask the girls. 'Sies, traffic cops have become so cheap. Next time you'll just have to dole them fish and chips, they'll let you free.'

On the corner of Plein Street where a man in his thirties, looking swell in made-in-Thailand Levi's, is busy watering the pavement with kilolitres of piss. I look disapprovingly at him. He turns around.

'Why are you looking at me? Are you one of those gay men? Do you get fascinated looking at other men?'

'No,' I say, 'bhuti wam, why are you urinating in the street?'

He utters unprintables. I can't catch what he says, something to do with human anatomy, but you can tell when someone's not wishing you nice things. 'Voetsek!' he finally says. 'What are you, police? You educated types se niyang nyanyisa. Why don't you go to the suburbs where the likes of you live with whites! Ungazontshela. Wena ubani? I piss wherever I wish, swine.' I sense danger. Dash away quickly. Why should I die for Jo'burg?

This, I can't help it, is bound to be controversial, especially when black people have been told time and again by apartheid that they are dirty, animalistic and useless. But I have to ask, with all due respect: Bafowethu – why is it that we seem to be littering and soiling ourselves, reducing our areas of domination to ruin? Of course, the council needs to clean up or be cleaned out. Shopkeepers pay expensive rent. All of us pay skyrocketing taxes.

Why is it that we contribute to this dirty image, playing right into the destructive images that are being heaped on us? Besides sex workers, I can count only five white people here. The only faces I see, some gleaming with pride, others masking suffering, are black people's. Can't we wake and smell the coffee? Our daily surroundings are so dirty we don't even see them any more. This must come to a screeching stop.

Yes, some of us use very apocalyptic terms. But look around Johannesburg: there is a riot going on. Frank talk: Johannesburg needs effective implementation of the law. Those caught dirtying or ignoring dirt should be punished. Siestog, Johannesburg! Phoaarr, bare hao hlape. You are like a pigsty!

Bongani Madondo, 32, is a senior staff writer at Sunday World. He also writes for the New York based leftwing journal 1st of the Month and has contributed to Mail & Guardian, City Press, True Love and the Sunday Times Lifestyle Magazine. A longer version of this piece orginally appeared in the Mail & Guardian.

aftertears

Kgafela oa Magogodi

121 gun salute
in avalon cemetery
we carry our hearts
in hand
wave them in the air
pistol style
pump action weep fashion
pull the trigger
bullets pop soda tears
jumpstart the dead
with the loud sounds
of our mourning

aftertears
we cry in style
we say
lefu la hao le ya mphidisa

it's
a hanky panky party
jammin'
in the name of the dead

Kgafela oa Magogodi is a poet, lyricist, film scholar, screenwriter and lecturer based at the Wits School of Arts, University of the Witwatersrand. He is a seasoned performer. A collection of his poems, including 'aftertears', was published as *Thy Condom Come* in 2000.

The changing faces of Jo'burg

Arthur Maimane

Apartheid forced me into self-imposed exile – OK, I ran away from The Struggle – as a young, hotshot journalist believing I knew it all. I was one of the first of the adventurous breed who worked on revolutionary *Drum* magazine and created what nostalgia now terms 'the golden age of black journalism'. I had to know it all to survive in a fast and hard-living society that didn't forgive mistakes but exploited them. I was, in township slang, a klevah: one of the 'wake-up' majita on the inside track – a denizen of Jo'burg, Jozi, Gauteng, Egoli.

We took our pick of a favourite name for the city of gold because that choice marked who you were. An insider, outsider or on the fringes of a violent, multiracial society. Some insisted they were European without ever having been there; some of us were classified natives, but warned the land wasn't our own; others were termed coloured as if the rest didn't have any colour. Outsiders fresh out of the bundu were moegoes. 'Jim Comes to Jo'burg' types as portrayed in the seminal movie of that title: wide-eyed and marvelling at skyscrapers and the many wonders of a fabled city.

I thought I knew it all until decades later, when it was safe to return home to a land that was about to be our own. Then I realised that this once-upon-a-time klevah was now as ignorant as those Jims. I'd never really known much about the city – nobody ever had, I realised, and that was a reason for the various names for this economic capital of the country.

My knowledge of the city as a wake-up majita of the Kofifi era was really only a blinkered view of one part of society. And I had abandoned that in favour of even greater cities north of the equator. Now I have the freedom to explore and actually live in those enclaves where once the only black people tolerated were domestic servants. In the old days, we could only glimpse the suburbs we called 'the avenues' in the light of day. We saw luxurious houses on tree-lined streets on the routes our commuter buses thundered along into the city. And all we knew of that city was what was necessary for us to hustle for tiny bits of the gold that was supposed to pave the streets.

We didn't know 'the real' Jo'burg of verdant valleys above the gold reefs that bulged into ridges, hills and rocky koppies. We didn't know the quiet, tree-lined streets that were 'white by night' and restful, scenic panoramas at all times. What we knew as officially mere 'temporary sojourners' were flat, treeless dustbowls once called 'locations' before their upliftment to 'townships' by apartheid's spin doctors.

The townships and shack non-cities have mushroomed in my absence. Soweto was my final home but is now at least a dozen times larger than the Orlando I roamed before exile, when squatters lived in Masakeng – shacks made of sacking and much more miserable than us living in matchbox houses.

But now I'm a moegoe who gets lost in those exclusive enclaves and the city centre amazed this returnee: it boasts real skyscrapers instead of the thirteen-storey Anstey's Building that was once the pride of Jo'burg. That solitary structure was replaced by the Carlton Centre that claimed to be the tallest in Africa.

All my remembered landmarks have disappeared as completely as the Sophiatown we called Kofifi with rundown shops and slum housing. The new danger is not being arrested or mugged but driving against several lines of fast-moving traffic along streets with familiar names that are now one-way thoroughfares.

On my second return in 1994 the president of a democratic state was Nelson Mandela and a white friend remarked: 'It's different now, isn't it? A real African city!'

The city of gold had turned black. There were hardly any white faces on streets which teemed with Africans weaving their tricky way around vendors who clogged the pavements. Eloff Street was no longer the main drag once lined by the smartest stores on the continent. They had fled to the suburban shopping malls where white residents live in voluntary exile, fearing the violent crime waves which drown the old central business area. What had once glittered with apparitions of gold had, as some of these internal exiles would say, gone to the dogs. But crime has followed them to Sandton City and other new centres of choice for the best in life.

But there is hopeful transformation too: black suburbanites and children of different colours and races are schoolmates and making friendships that are personal and not simply a result of enforced political correctness. I'm still puzzled by white women leading black toddlers by the hand in shopping malls and carrying babies on their hips. Are these children – 'piccaninnies' of my own youth – adopted or the offspring of madam's maid? Such a madam would never have dared be seen doing that in the days before her own liberation.

Arthur Maimane worked in east and west Africa and in London for Reuters, the BBC and Independent Television News. He returned twice to South Africa for *The Weekly Mail* and *The Star*. He now writes books.

Jo'burg Lovesong

Rian Malan

What's good to say about Johannesburg? I enquired as we drove through a storm towards our dinner. 'Well,' said Kate, 'there's the weather, the weather and the weather.' But it had been raining for days, so the proposition seemed dubious at present. We drove on in silence, racking our brains. Steve mumbled something about the plethora of golf courses, but drew no takers. The contessa mentioned street markets, where you can buy artefacts from all over Africa, but someone pointed out that many were fake. As we took our seats in a restaurant called the Smokestack, Steve made a case for South Africa's excellent red wines. I could drink to that, but they're made around Cape Town, so they don't really count.

Stumped, we sipped our cabernet and looked around. The restaurant was brand new and very larney, as we say here, larney meaning fashionable and expensive. The decor was bare bricks and rough-hewn finishes – rather New York 1980s, with a clientele to match: slender young women in designer silks, fat-cats in suits and ponytails, and the races mixed in proportions comfortably familiar to Americans. A row of BMWs and Porsches was visible through the plate glass windows. Everyone had straight teeth, strong bodies and radiant self-confidence, and you could bet they all had servants to pick up behind them.

Ja, well, *plus ça change* and all that. Jo'burg has always been world-famous for its vulgar displays of greed and ostentation. I spent the first few decades of my life longing to see the place engulfed by the fires of revolution, but the struggle petered out into a mannered bourgeois transformation, and here we were, ten years later, the loyal subjects of Mandela and Mbeki, and richer than ever. The stock market and the IT sector are running wild. The freeways are clogged with gleaming new chariots. Property prices are rising, while crime threatens to stabilise. For the lucky few, life is more perfect than ever. The same cannot be said for the rain-soaked beggars lining the streets outside, arms waving like sea anemones, trying to earn a few cents by guiding the next Mercedes into a parking bay.

Johannesburg has always been ruled by grasping elites, and civilised visitors have always recoiled in horror from our vacuous excesses, branding the city one of the ugliest on the planet. Looking back, nobody ever really loved this place except the Voortrekkers, who arrived on covered wagons in the spring of 1837. After trekking for months across harsh, dry plains, they spied a ridge on the horizon, its flanks streaked by gushing streams, hence the name Witwatersrand, or ridge of white waters. As they drew nearer, clouds of birds rose from marshes, and great herds of antelope thundered away across the savannah. They were on the roof of Africa, almost six thousand feet high; the sun was hot but the air was cool, and the veld was carpeted with wild flowers. The Boers thought they'd arrived in paradise, so they staked out farms, built homesteads out of mud and reed and idled away the next five decades in a bucolic swoon, blissfully unaware that they were sitting on top of the world's richest gold reef.

The gold was discovered in 1886, and the Boers were instantly overrun by a greed-maddened stampede of Cockney navvies and British imperialists, American freebooters, French brothel-keepers and German Jews. In their wake came Russians, Latvians, indentured Indians, Chinese coolies and armies of sullen Africans, forced off the land by hut taxes. A great city rose out of nowhere. Ziggurats leaped skyward. Mine shafts went down a mile. Fabulous fortunes were made, and fortune-seekers kept coming. In my youth, the racial scientists of apartheid tried to hold back the tide and turn the city into a whites-only moonbase on Africa, a mad undertaking that came to nothing. The Boers were undermined, overthrown by Mandela and cast on to the trash heap of history, whereupon the invasion resumed apace.

Peasants decamped from the countryside and settled in shacks around the city. Armies of cheerful opportunists flooded in from elsewhere in Africa – Malians, Ethiopians, gregarious Nigerians, *personnes de élégance* from Francophone lands. Serbs invaded the cafés of Yeoville. Pockets of Hillbrow became French-speaking. Cyrildene was colonised by traders from Beijing, and the best suburbs have of course been settled by our new ruling class, 'Afristocrats' and politicians who tool around in BMWs and dine in the Smokestack. I pushed my plate aside, daunted by the thought of having to explain why anyone would become attached to such a place.

Well, for a start, there's the weather, clear and crisp in winter, with skies of startling blue, and soft warm springs giving way to burning summers punctuated by violent African thunderstorms. To walk through the aftermath of such a deluge is amazing. The streets are strewn with mauve flowers knocked off the jacaranda trees. Great clouds of red and pink bougainvillaea billow over high garden walls, forming a psychedelic arch over the old stone alley that winds up the ridge behind my house. From the summit, it's as if a pastel mist is drifting across the suburbs.

Two decades of convulsive change notwithstanding, aspects of the sweet white life persist down there – the thwock of balls on tennis courts, the click of woods on bowling greens, the clink of ice in frosted glasses borne on trays by loyal African servants. My little corner of the city remains rather British, with Anglican churches, friendly grocers and a ratepayers' association full of crabby ex-Rhodesians and old Africa hands who rail in vain about unkempt pavements, broken street lamps and other signs of the supposedly inevitable slide into anarchy. But all is not lost; not yet. You can still get French pastries and Austrian coffee in the fashionable boîtes of Melville, on the far side of the yonder golf course, and the Westcliff Hotel still serves a tolerable cucumber sandwich with afternoon tea. And that, sadly, is about as far as the bourgeoisie ventures, because it's a jungle out there – one of the most dangerous cities in the world. But also one of the most interesting, if you have the courage to go.

When visitors from outside want to know why I live here, I always take them into the decaying heart of our old downtown, where Africa and the West come face to face across a narrow street called Diagonal. On one side there's a little African apothecary where a certain K Naidoo does a roaring trade in healing and magical herbs, baboon skulls, lizard feet and tiny vials of crocodile fat. On the other, there's a soaring edifice of blue glass and steel, designed by Helmut Jahn, the great avant-garde architect from Chicago.

I've been there a hundred times, and the juxtaposition has never ceased to amaze and elate me – witch doctors entering one building, accountants exiting the other, and mingling on the street between. It seems extraordinary, but it isn't, because this is the nature of the city: at once an outpost of western 'civilisation' and a point of entry into another reality, a parallel kingdom of African consciousness. Prophets dance around fires in the shadow of skyscrapers. Ancestral cattle sacrifices are conducted in suburban gardens. Mud huts and nuclear power stations occur in the same landscape. University professors smear lion fat on their faces as they set forth to settle faculty battles. In the cafés of Hillbrow, exiles from thirty African nations gather to plot coups and comebacks in undertones.

Which is not to say that all Africans are refugees or mystics. The city teems with black merchant bankers and nuclear physicists, black rugby players, black teenagers in the uniforms of colonial Etons called Saint this or King that, speaking English with the same plummy accents as their white classmates, and subscribing to identical values. I once had an African friend who defined hell as 'a place where really bad blacks are sent to spend eternity discussing cricket with white men'. His daughter, a sparkling yuppie of twenty-three, thinks hell is discussing Africa with me, when she would rather be shopping or dancing to kwaito, the Americanised hip-hop, often sung in Afrikaans, the language of apartheid, by township youths with baseball caps on backwards.

Myself, I remain attached to more traditional musics. It's an indescribable pleasure to tool around the city with the car radio blaring, listening to mbqanga on this station or mbube on that, with Boer concertina music between. The ether is full of strange languages. The pavements are clogged with alfresco barbershops in the Ghanaian style and traders from Zanzibar and Timbuktu. When the sun goes down, we set forth to eat and drink from the smorgasbord brought here by our many invaders. You can dine on mopani worms and English roast beef, pasta and curry, Congolese delicacies, Mozambican peri-peri and absolutely authentic Szechuan cuisine in the People's Republic of Cyrildene. If you're still standing, you can repair to Melville in the small hours and debate with black-jacketed intellectuals in a miasma of liquor fumes and marijuana smoke. You might get hijacked on your way home, but what the heck.

If it is true, as Buddhist sages maintain, that materialism coarsens the spirit and that life itself is an illusion, Jo'burg is a fine place to pursue enlightenment. Theft is so common that it's hardly worth mentioning. Everyone knows someone who was murdered. You either allow the danger to poison your psyche and deaden your soul, or you learn to be brave, and laugh at the prospect of your own annihilation. It's not necessarily kin to wisdom, but it's a fine quality anyway. I love Jo'burgers. They're loud and vulgar, and the worst of them will shoot you or embezzle your trust fund if you don't watch your back, but they all have something the Boer poet Breytenbach called 'heartspace'. It comes from living on adrenalin, which is, of course, the intoxicant that keeps us here, or draws us back if we try to escape.

And we all come back, eventually. My life here is full of returnees. An old poet who used to knock around Tangier with William Burroughs. An ex-terrorist who blew up a nuclear power station. A webmaster who abandoned a career in Silicon Valley. An ex-Oxford professor. Foreigners think we're nuts, coming back to a doomed city on a damned continent, but there's something you don't understand: it's boring where you are. You'll probably live longer than us and acquire more possessions, but there's no ferment in your societies, no excitement, no edge. Your newspapers are bland and your politics are inconsequential, so many storms in teacups. You want crises? We've got real ones – Aids, forty per cent unemployment, the highest rape and murder rates on the planet and a government that wants to put blacks in our national rugby team, just on principle. We're talking stuff that's really worth fighting about, with real fire in the belly. We're talking about a country where life is an insane gamble that'll end in blinding light or darkest disaster, and there's absolutely no way of knowing which.

We yaw between terror and ecstasy. Every day is an adventure. The only constant is the weather, the African sun that beats down on our backs as we potter around in the garden, digging up rich African soils all red with oxides and squirmy with earthworms. Our tomatoes are fat and red. Our Swiss chard grows like trees. Towards evening, we walk the dogs up the old stone path to the crest of the ridge to watch the sun go down. Flights of sacred ibis cross the sky. Lions roar in the zoo nearby. Police chase hijackers on freeways, sirens screaming. We're in the wild heart of Jo'burg, and it's a pretty good place to be.

Rian Malan is a hack recently dragged to Cape Town by his foreign wife, who failed to grasp his fascination with the big mean city. He vows to return once she tires of the Cape's superficial prettiness. He is the author of the book *My Traitor's Heart*. 'Jo'burg Lovesong' was first published in the *Daily Telegraph*.

The Master of English

Johnny Masilela

During the turbulent 1970s, I was one of a pool of wannabe reporters based at the Pretoria Bureau of the legendary and now defunct *Rand Daily Mail*. Then came the day I was required to knock together a review on the stage production of a Shakespeare play. I was required to explain to the reader what kind of attire the cast was wearing, particularly the baggy trousers folks used to don during the best and worst of the Bard's times. As a young and inexperienced reporter, I got stuck trying to figure out what the hell those people wore in those olden days, so I decided to seek the advice of our bureau chief, Benardi Wessels.

Benardi had no idea himself what the baggy trousers were called.

'Why don't you try the Master of English?' Wessels suggested.

'Who's that?' I enquired.

'Call Johannesburg head office and ask to speak to Doc Bikitsha,' was his reply.

So I picked up the phone, introduced myself to Bro Doc, and asked him the big question.

'Pantaloops!' was Bro Doc's reply.

And that was my first encounter with Bro Doc, otherwise known as Carcass by his contemporaries from as early as the days of the great *Drum* writers of the 1950s.

After a few more months at the Pretoria Bureau, Benardi arranged for me to move to Johannesburg, where Bro Doc took me under his wing. I remember vividly when Bro Doc saw me for the first time, he whispered something to another ol' man river of black journalism, Harold Pongolo (may your soul rest in peace, Bro HP). Bro Doc said to Bro HP: 'This laaitie from Pretoria with the light complexion, is he Khoisan or something?' Bro HP was not a man who laughed often, but that day he nearly tumbled over his chair with mirth.

Bro Doc is in retirement now, but the legacy of the Master of English lives on. Some time ago I was working on something which required me to name this wooden thing which stands on four legs, balancing the chalkboard of the olden days, the thing on which artists place their canvas. I telephoned fellow artist Gomolemo Mokae, who apologised that he was about to go into a meeting. 'Why don't you call the Master of English?' Mokae suggested.

'Let's start from the beginning,' said Bro Doc when I phoned him. The artist, he said, holds a brush and something shaped like a kidney. 'This thing is called a palette, p-a-l-e-t-t-e. The palette has holes like the inkpot, which contain different paint colours. This other thing you're talking about, that balances the chalkboard, is called the easel, e-a-s-e-l. I hope that answers your question, ol' chap.'

The Master of English had spoken! Is it surprising that I asked Doc Bikitsha to write the endorsement on the back jacket of my debut novel?

Johnny Masilela is the author of *We Shall Not Weep*. He is the News Editor at the *Sunday Sun* and a screenwriter whose short film 'Christmas With Granny' won the MNet New Directions Film Award.

Soweto: Fragment from a homecoming

John Matshikiza

Wake up in shock, after barely an hour's sleep in my long-lost cousin's house. Pain and itching round my neck, on my back, both arms.

Blistering barnacles – bedbugs! Reality is beginning to bite, literally. This homecoming, this familiarity as I set foot on my native turf for the first time in thirty-two years, is breeding contempt among the locals.

I've snapped on the bedside light and slap and scratch at myself, reach myopically for my glasses and search the bed-clothes in terror, wondering what a bedbug will look like when I see it, and will I be able to handle it? Look around the little room. My cousin's bedroom, my first night here in deep Soweto, the room much smaller now in the sharp, unromantic focus of the small hours.

This is Soweto, boy, where you ran away from. The walls are yellow and sooty. Things are packed in cardboard boxes alongside and on top of the shabby old wardrobe, the tiny desk is useless as a desk, it is a bedside table and store-cupboard, the government has built hovels for the people, and the people are trapped in them, shoulder to shoulder, step out of your front door and how can you avoid seeing your neighbour knifing her husband in the gloom of her stoep because she's gone crazy, or Sherry in the broad daylight of that very afternoon being chased down the street by must-be a hundred Bushies, grinning and waving sticks in anticipation of a little variation in this cruel life, all wanting to take part in corrective, instant punishment of Sherry, 'cos she, this middle-aged seventeen-year-old, had the audacity to leave her two-year-old and the baby with her ninety-year-old father who's a drunk, alone and without food and milk from her horrified breasts for three whole days, looking to fit some fun into the weekend and make it last a little longer.

Here's Sherry running barefoot past my cousin's stoep, and the 'community', from four to sixty, running hopefully after her with sticks.

They corner her down in the spruit, where Mr Snit, the municipal policeman, found that snake in '59 and couldn't resist bringing it all the way up the hill in a sack to terrorise us kids playing in the yard of my grandmother's crèche where we used to while away our useless, childish hours. The crèche is still there, on the corner over Mlamlankhunzi, just as I left it, with regrets. So anyway, Mr Snit let the snake writhe before our eyes while Grandma wasn't looking, and then burned it, in its death throes, in front of us, with fire. What the hell were we supposed to make of it all? Aged four? Memories of a time before exile.

Flash forward to this afternoon. The dust rises from around the spruit as they lay into Sherry. They finally caught her and are telling her what's what, no matter how bad they all are.

Jesus said: 'Who dares to throw the first stone?'

'Me,' say all the Bushies, voluntarily.

This is Soweto, Johannesburg. We go back to what we were doing. Watching television, drinking beer, talking politics. Staring like into a mirror at the identical township pouring away in every direction over the rounded hills.

This must have been a beautiful landscape, once, until they discovered the gold. The piles of mine dumps, left there for the township to crouch around, the white man's dirt abandoned where he decided he was finished with it, the skeletons of mine headgear rusting over sucked-out shafts where the coloureds can fall in if they want to, I've got work to do . . .

That was all earlier in the day. Now the house is sleeping. In the quiet house I am alone with invisible bedbugs. I scratch and slap my skin, hoping someone will wake up and come and keep me company. Nothing.

Prepare for sleep again. Just drawing the sheet up to my chin, gingerly, when, damn me, if the fattest thing, big and brown like a two-cent coin, doesn't come marching out of the folds of my cousin's blanket and stride straight towards my face. I haven't even switched off the light. I am shocked. It's so fucking big. Stamping across the white sheets, out of nowhere, fearing nothing.

I clap the sheet hard. Hold it, breathing heavily. How do you kill a bedbug? An axe? I open the fold a crack. There he is still, squirming. Released, he starts marching again, straight for my jugular. I squeeze the sheet tight, twist it, grind, dig my fingernails into the patch where he is, in there where I can't see his ugly township mug and don't want to. Me and him, the same.

Fearfully, gingerly, release my grip. Peer into the folds, my knuckles white. My blood seeps out of him and his mangled body, smearing the sheet. And that terrible, sweet smell they always said bedbugs give off when you squash them.

He's dead. I look around the room. Why? This has all

already been written by guys like Casey Motsitsi. Why do I have to go through it in person?

Didn't sleep any more.

Groggy for the big indaba planned for the next day. Indaba of very old people, here in my cousin's house, singing hymns for me. The legendary Peter Rezant at my side on the broken sofa, telling me tales about people from way back. Can you believe it? A wonderful prayer in Xhosa from tall, rumpled Uncle Nick, thanking Thixo and Somandla for my return to the land of my ancestors. Food, food, food, beer. The girls in the kitchen with all their children. How can these children tell whom they belong to? Communalism gone wild. Home.

I swear I am not going to sleep another night in that bed. If Gideon doesn't show up to rescue me like he promised, I'll phone Nadine Gordimer, Rian Malan, anyone from the other side in comforting, white-white Johannesburg, just to be able to lie down in the manner to which I have become accustomed.

Soweto? Haikona, jong!

John Matshikiza was born in Johannesburg and grew up in Lusaka and London, where he worked in theatre, television and film as an actor, director and writer, before returning to South Africa in 1991. He has produced and directed television documentaries and drama in Johannesburg, and is currently a columnist for the *Mail & Guardian*.

Outsiders

Zakes Mda

It would be wrong to say nothing has changed since liberation in 1994. Although the squatter camps have become much bigger because the new rulers abolished influx control laws that prohibited black people from coming to Johannesburg unless they were employed, the government is working hard to house the homeless. New low-income houses are coming up where it used to be nothing but veld. Or where it used to be makeshift corrugated iron and cardboard shelters in the middle of a quagmire. The government gives the homeless people, who are either unemployed or who receive too small an income to afford accommodation, a subsidy to build their own houses. Some people have criticised this state welfarism because it creates a dependency mentality among the poor. They tend to look to the government to provide them with everything. The government carries on with its housing pro- gramme, and thousands of previously homeless people now have houses of their own. Still the government, with its meagre resources, is not able to house everybody. The homeless are still the bane of the inner city.

Unemployment and homelessness have tended to cause a lot of xenophobia among the poor Johannesburgers. The scapegoat is always the foreigner. Everyone who looks vaguely like a foreigner is regarded as an illegal immigrant. Especially if they are darker in complexion than the 'average South African' – whatever that means. South Africa's xenophobia is really racism. South Africans – both black and white – don't hate and fear all foreigners. Only black foreigners from the rest of Africa and from the United States of America. White foreigners from Europe and the Americas are welcomed with open arms. The impression that is created is that black foreigners come to steal local jobs whereas white foreigners are bringing investment into the country.

This, of course, is a fallacy born of South Africa's old apartheid past. Black South Africans long internalised self-hate. Hence their mistrust and suspicion of fellow black Africans. The government and non-governmental organisations that are run by the more enlightened South Africans are trying very hard to fight this attitude. Of course most members of the government were in exile in other countries in Africa where they received assistance to fight their war of liberation. They therefore are embarrassed by their compatriots' xenophobia. Many campaigns continue to be waged through the mass media to wean the people of Johannesburg and South Africa from this xenophobia.

One big fallacy is that black foreigners come to Johannesburg to steal jobs from the locals. Many people from the north of South Africa come to this country as political refugees. Many of them are professional people who nevertheless don't get jobs in their professions. Instead they create jobs for themselves. It is not unusual to drive into a shopping mall in one of the suburbs of Johannesburg and find that the parking attendants are lawyers or teachers from Congo. Or from any of the French-speaking countries of central and west Africa.

One of these lawyers was my shoemaker at a street corner in Melville. Although he learned shoe repairing as an emergency when he arrived in Johannesburg and couldn't get a job in his profession, he managed to do it well. Many people brought their shoes to him. Soon he employed other people. Now he runs a big store of his own, selling all sorts of locally made and imported shoes. That is how many of the foreigners from the African countries start. They are very enterprising. They are not afraid to start doing menial jobs that locals are loath to touch. Then they grow and end up creating employment for the very South Africans who despise them.

Gold in the streets of Johannesburg may be an illusion for many South Africans who flock into this city from other towns and villages, but many foreigners from the rest of Africa have found it through their hard work and enterprising spirit. They have found it in the businesses that they have established from zero. Businesses that end up employing many South Africans.

Zanemvula Kizito Gatyeni (better known as Zakes) Mda is an award-winning playwright and novelist. He is the author of three novels – Ways of Dying, She Plays with the Darkness, The Heart of Redness – as well as several anthologies of plays and a volume of poetry.

Jozi-Jozi, City of Dreams

Gcina Mhlope

I first saw Johannesburg in my dreams. Oh, the thousands of shiny tall buildings, happy, fast-talking people who had everything they wanted, the fancy cars playing the latest music and, yes, the millions of lights that turned any night into day! At least that is what we heard from those who had been to the mining city of gold, where the hills echo like thunder and delicious meat of every kind is always available, until your teeth can't chew any more.

Who could resist longing for such a place? I looked at the migrant workers who came back to our small town so polished, their skins glowing, their shoes shiny and their clothes telling the whole story even before the people themselves said anything.

I remember the hushed silence as we listened to stories about the place where many sons and daughters simply disappeared forever. Many of them died in the mines, no doubt, but others just could not bear the old-fashioned lifestyles, looking after livestock, tilling the land, walking for many kilometres under the burning sun and, of course, watching their families starve as they waited for rains. Those sons and daughters preferred to stay in the city of gold, to carve a new life for themselves. Some even changed their names and became untraceable.

I was in my late teens when I first went to Johannesburg with my sister. To say I was excited is an understatement. I was delirious with joy. My heart was beating very fast and my mind was racing with all the images I had been fed. The bus journey was long but I did not care: to finally see Johannesburg was enough for me. And when we passed Germiston and headed for the big city itself, I heard the parents and other relatives noisily waking up the sleeping children so they could see the millions of lights that shone like stars.

It was as if there were two sets of stars, those up in the sky and then the ones shining on the ground. Everything was spread out there as we alighted from the bus and went to board another to Dunkeld, Rosebank. It was all a dream. I could not stop smiling. What a place!

Well, many things happened during those first few days and weeks to make my holiday so special I wanted to sing. But the gold on the streets was just not shiny, the places I was not allowed to visit were too many, and the whys I asked were straining my relationships. Above all, the police vans put fear into our hearts even when we knew we were no criminals. But I am glad that I grew to like Johannesburg for other reasons that were very real. I could see the good and the bad. I connected with like-minded young people and I shared my dreams as an artist.

Johannesburg has been the city of gold, yes, but to the miners and their families with humiliating salaries and demeaning treatment, death, tears were the order of the day. Their wives never knew the feeling of wearing a golden ring or necklace.

But to us it was the heart of the artistic world where everything happened. Working in magazines, radio and then in theatre and TV – these experiences were to shape my life. The most talented musicians, actors, writers, artists of all kinds could fulfil their dreams in this city. It was the place where you could meet influential people and be launched on to the stages of the world.

Being in the right place at the right time, as they say. In the years I worked in Johannesburg I often saw extremely talented people shuffling through their dreams and chuckling coldly as hope slipped through their fingers like a wet piece of soap.

Of course the city centre is nothing like the place I was awed by in 1979. In those days African people were not to be seen in the city centre after hours. Today the tables are turned, though not by law. Then, life dealt me and my people such stinking cards. I had to struggle very hard to chase hatred out of my heart – to say 'get out, there is no room for you here!'

But through all this, Jozi-Jozi never took away the values I was brought up with. 'Respect yourself and those you meet along the way, and you'll be all right anywhere.' That was my father's advice and I will never forget it. And hard work? Well, that's my middle name. I must have inherited it from both my parents.

Gcina Mhlope has been writing and performing on stage and screen for the past twenty-one years. She has written many children's books as well as adult audience poetry, short stories and plays. Her writings have been published all over the world and translated into German, French, Italian, Swahili and Japanese.

Jo'burg idolised and scorned

Andrew Molefe

Jo'burg, Egoli, Gauteng, Jozi, Mbiza – whatever name you use for Africa's media, finance, communications and commerce hub, mention of the city evokes strong reactions among non-residents. Mention any of the above names to anyone outside Gauteng Province and I bet my last battered rand that you're bound to attract both negative and positive attention. Some people will look at you with admiration and envy; others might be scornful.

Many cities attract mixed reactions. Frank Sinatra captured the highs and lows of New York City in his immortal song, 'New York, New York'. Miriam Makeba did the same for Johannesburg with her heart-wrenching 'Gauteng', while Hugh Masekela waxed lyrical about the city of gold on the tracks 'Stimela' and 'Going to Johannesburg'.

A few years ago, I travelled the length and breadth of southern Africa as a journalist-cum-show promoter. One day colleague Jonathan Coetzee and I found ourselves in a small village café in Botswana. Back in Jo'burg in those days, it was fashionable for liberal whites to shave their heads in a tradition made popular by the pantsulas of the time. In rural Botswana, the appearance of a tall, thickset white man sporting a chiskop and trotting behind a lean black man must have been quite a sight.

As a cosmopolitan pair, Coetzee and I stuck out like a sore thumb in the ramshackle café that sold hot steaks and luke-warm coffee. At the height of apartheid in the 1980s, the world thought that ordinary blacks and whites were always donnering each other. They thought us incapable of forming friendships or business partnerships across the colour bar.

An aged, wrinkly Motswana, clad in priest's dog collar and flowing, ankle-length cassock approached us. After sizing us up, he asked where we came from. 'Johannesburg,' I replied in my Jo'burg accent. For a split second there was a mixture of fear and loathing in his eyes. Then, with trembling hands, he turned around and hurried away, without another word. I still ask myself: what went into the man's head at the mere mention of Johannesburg?

But my Jo'burg roots once saved my life in Brixton in London, when some riff-raff tried to mug me. It was my South African English and a trick I used that saved me. I told the ruffians that I lived a street from Mandela's house. Can you believe it! Even lowlifes from across the oceans hold Madiba in high esteem.

While still on the subject of the up side of Johannesburg, let me tell you about my uncle Joe 'Blanket' Molefe, who I consider to be among the last Mohicans, the real McCoys.

Joe was born into a poor rural family in Manana, a farming area near Lichtenburg in North West Province. When he was about nine years, and with only two years of education, Uncle

Joe ran away from home to Johannesburg. Years later he told me: 'When I saw the tall buildings, beautifully dressed people and the shining cars, I said to myself: "Ah, Joe, this is it. This is the promised land. I will never go to bed hungry again".'

My uncle is now in his late seventies, having never worked for a white man. He has survived by his wits, and still changes his white shirts twice a day. When he rattles his rheumatic bones, he still puts on his designer jersey, a scarf and a long coat.

Johannesburg has been good to him all these years. But for every Joe 'Blanket', there are thousands of others to whom the streets of Johannesburg have been nothing but boulevards of broken dreams.

Andrew Molefe has been a journalist for the past twenty years. He is a regular contributor to the Sunday Independent as a literary critic, writes a weekly series on Johannesburg for the Sunday Sun, and is Africa correspondent for the international news magazine Global Vision. 'Jo'burg Idolised and Scorned' appeared in the first issue of the Sunday Sun in January 2002.

Poetry on the train

Kobus Moolman

My heart sank when the compartment door was drawn back and I saw my room for the twelve-hour trip home. It was already occupied. Well, no problem, I thought to myself. Coming up to Jo'burg on the train I had been faced with the same problem. I had simply asked the conductor if I could change and he had found me a cabin where I could be on my own; to think my own thoughts, laugh out loud at my pettiness and, most importantly, write without distraction, all night if I chose.

Of course things had been considerably easier on that occasion: my proposed companion had been an elderly white man who smoked like a steam engine and had the watery eyes and puffy nose of a heavy drinker. This time I would have to make excuses for not wanting to share a cabin with a quiet, middle-aged black man.

We greeted each other cordially and after some idle exchanges I explained to him why I preferred to be alone and would be seeking a cabin of my own. I think he understood. Then the conductor came around. He was a thin African man with a woollen skullcap of sorts, and, judging from the questions fired icily at me, he definitely misinterpreted my request. It was going to be fruitless to try to persuade him. I gave up and resigned myself to a dull and early night. I only hoped my companion wasn't going to try and talk to me all the way home.

He introduced himself as Hezlon Khaya Xolo from Soweto. He had two children. The firstborn was fourteen and the last was eight. He was on his way to a small rural village inland from Port Shepstone to visit his parents and his brothers. He worked for Spoornet, and this was his annual free pass. He worked in the shunting yards, and he told me how difficult and dangerous this type of work was. Several of his friends had lost a hand or even an entire limb. He had once witnessed a man chopped in half by a runaway truck, he said.

I wanted to prepare for a talk I was to give to a private school on writing poetry, so I gave my companion a copy of my newly published collection of poetry, *Time like Stone*, to read. Hezlon read for a long time in silence while I scribbled away in my notebook that rocked and jerked with the unpredictable motion of the train.

Finally Hezlon asked me what the title meant, and we discussed the burden of time, how I felt that it weighed like a stone upon us, and was impossible to shift. He nodded. He understood weight; the weight of a fully laden truck that was capable of slicing a careless man's head clean off his shoulders. Then he wanted to know how a poem came to me. Where did it come from? How did it happen? So we spoke of dreams, and of visions and nightmares; of things that stirred in one – without form or warning – and had to be obeyed or they would turn into poison and ruin us. Again, he understood.

Then he asked me if he could write something, and how he should do it. I said to him that he had to wait; that he could (and had to) prepare himself, like a boxer or a football player, that he needed to be in shape to be able to receive the poem and to handle it, but that he was not the origin of his poem. It chose him, he could not go out and seek it. Again he nodded, and fell silent. The black veld outside was pegged out like an animal skin to dry. The heavy forms of pylons and sombre trees lumbered past. A tin shack, an empty bridge. Then the black veld returned, seemingly impenetrable, seemingly endless.

'I've got it,' he suddenly said, and his face lit up with excitement. 'Silent rivers. Help me. Write it down.' So I opened my notebook (volume 52) and on a new page wrote the first line of Hezlon's own poem: 'Silent Rivers'.

Over the next three hours Hezlon's poem grew slowly from those first two words into a page-long meditation on the river of life that flowed in his veins, 'at a constant speed / without beginning / or ending'. At the end he was tired, but exultant. He made his bed soon after from some blankets he had with him and went to sleep. He was an honest man who led a simple and hard life. He was used to straightforward things like coupling coaches together, like handling a wrench or a spanner. He understood these things. And he had now come to understand his own kind of poetry.

I lay for a long time in the darkness of the cabin staring out the window at the impenetrable world beyond. I push with my mind so often against the surface of things that I exhaust and confuse myself. How? Why? What? But to no avail. Then a simple chance encounter in a train compartment breaks in upon us and all of a sudden the scales fall from our eyes, our hearts are laid open again and we feel once more how deeply we are connected with each other – if only we open ourselves to the unexpected.

Kobus Moolman writes feature articles for *The Natal Witness*. His debut collection of poetry, *Time like Stone*, was awarded the Ingrid Jonker Prize in 2001.

Welcome to our Hillbrow

Phaswane Mpe

Welcome to our Hillbrow . . .

Your first entry into Hillbrow, Refentše, was the culmination of many converging routes. You do not remember where the route first began. But you know all too well that the stories of migrants had a lot to do with its formation. By the time you left Tiragalong High School to come to the University of the Witwatersrand, at the dawn of 1991, you already knew that Hillbrow was a menacing monster, so threatening to its neighbours like Berea and downtown Johannesburg, that big, forward-looking companies were beginning to desert the inner city, heading for the northern suburbs such as Sandton. The lure of the monster was, however, hard to resist; Hillbrow has swallowed a number of the children of Tiragalong, who thought that the City of Gold was full of career opportunities for them.

One of the stories that you remember vividly was of a young man who died of a strange illness in 1990, when you were matriculating. The migrants said it could only have been Aids. After all, was he not often seen roaming the whore-houses and dingy pubs of Hillbrow? While his poor parents imagined that he was working away in the city, in order to make sure that there would be a huge bag of maize meal to send back for all at the homestead. The migrants, most of whom insisted that he was a stubborn brother, who suffered because of blocking his ears with gum while they dished out advice to him, also said that he was often seen with Makwerekwere women, hanging on to his arms and dazzling him with sugar-coated kisses that were sure to destroy any man, let alone an impressionable youngster like him.

He died, poor chap; of what precisely, no one knew. But strange illnesses courted in Hillbrow, as Tiragalong knew only too well, could only translate into Aids. This Aids, according to popular understanding, was caused by foreign germs that travelled down from the central and western parts of Africa. More specifically, certain newspaper articles attributed the source of the virus that caused Aids to a species called the Green Monkey, which people in some parts of west Africa were said to eat as meat, thereby contracting the disease. Migrants (who were Tiragalong's authoritative grapevine on all import-ant issues) deduced from such media reports that Aids's travel route into Johannesburg was through Makwerekwere; and Hillbrow was the sanctuary in which Makwerekwere basked.

There were others who went even further, saying that Aids was caused by the bizarre sexual behaviour of the Hillbrow-ans.

How could any man have sex with another man? they demanded to know.

Those who claimed to be informed – although none could admit to having seen or practised it personally – said such sex was done anally. They also explained how it was done – dog style – to the disgust of most of the people of Tiragalong, who insisted that filth and sex should be two separate things.

Surely, this large group argued, it was the shit that the greedy and careless penises sucked out of the equally eager anuses that could only lead to such dreadful illnesses?

Such were the scandalous stories that did the rounds on the informal migrant grapevine.

For formal news, there was Radio Lebowa – now Thobela FM – broadcasting snippets of car hijackings and robbers' shoot-outs with the Johannesburg Murder and Robbery Squad every news hour. Five men were found with their ribs ripped off by what appeared to have been a butcher's knife . . . Two women were raped and then killed in Quartz Street . . . Three Nigerians who evaded arrest at Jan Smuts Airport were finally arrested in Pretoria Street for drug dealing . . . Street kids, drunk with glue, brandy and wild visions of themselves as speeding Hollywood movie drivers, were racing their wire-made cars through red robots, thus increasingly becoming a menace to motorists driving through Hillbrow, especially in the vicinity of Banket and Claim Streets . . . At least eight people died and thirteen were seriously injured when the New Year's Eve celebrations took the form of torrents of bottles gushing out of the brooding clouds that were flat balconies . . . Men going anywhere near the corner of Quartz and Smit Streets were advised to beware of the menace of increasingly aggressive prostitutes . . . a few men had allegedly been raped there recently . . .

Welcome to our Hillbrow . . .

Phaswane Mpe, an author, lives in Johannesburg. His family live in the north of South Africa, very near Tiragalong. His poems and short stories have been published in several magazines. This extract comes from *Welcome to our Hillbrow*, his first novel, which was published in 2001.

Out of the mouths of babes

Samson Mulugeta

I exulted in my move to South Africa a year ago. My then two-year-old son, an Ethiopian-American, would grow up amidst the rich cultural and racial mosaic that is the new South Africa.

A year later, a year spent in one of Johannesburg's northern suburbs, our little brown boy appeared painfully out of place in a lily-white world.

There were small signs of Teddy's heightened racial consciousness within a few months of our arrival. Upon returning from his almost all-white nursery, he would yell 'Same hair Daddy, we have the same hair!' as he rubbed my wiry head with his tiny palm.

We had chosen his mostly Jewish school because we felt it would be more diverse, and because my wife liked the easy-going atmosphere after visiting the place. Soon she was part of a five-member mothers' group that met weekly, and two, three times a week Teddy was joined by other children from the group to drag his Thomas the Tank Engine set around our house.

The mothers in the group, among whom were an architect, a travel agent and a writer, led busy lives, and my wife was at the centre of a whirlwind of play dates, birthday parties and trips to the zoo.

We were aware that all of Teddy's close friends were white, and we figured he would take it in his stride.

But we became seriously worried after my wife had this conversation with Teddy one day on the way home from school.

'Guess what, Teddy? A man named Joe is going to come to our house to fix my car.'

'Is Joe black or white?'

'He is brown.'

'I don't like Joe.'

'Why?'

'Because brown people will kill you.'

'Who told you that?'

'Michael.'

Teddy adored Michael, a sandy-haired future rugby player, and imitated his every move. ('Teddy, don't pick your nose.' 'But Mommy, Michael picks his nose.')

We later traced the story to Michael's older sister, who goes to another school where the parents of four of her class-mates were recent victims of car hijackings.

Not being psychologists, my wife and I were unsure what all this meant. Around the house, we went out of our way not to identify people by their race. Some of our friends were black, but it was a fact that ninety per cent of the people our son met in his daily life were white.

The problem was compounded for us as expatriate blacks with no family support to draw on, unlike the local Africans.

Until we find a permanent solution our only hope of giving

182

our son a wider experience would appear to be our annual home leave trip to America.

Shame, as they say in South Africa.

Samson Mulugeta is the Africa Correspondent for *Newsday* in New York. He lives in Johannesburg.

The Revolution – through a glass darkly

Christopher Munnion

Not for the first time, nor for the last, there was blood on the floor of the Guildhall Executive Bar and Grill. Clutching a handkerchief to an ugly head wound, the middle-aged man had staggered off Market Street, up the stairs to one of Johannesburg's oldest hostelries and asked politely if he could use the phone.

Bruno, the Italian proprietor, insisted that he lie down and ordered up clean napkins to help staunch the flow of blood, at the same time telling the receptionist to call an ambulance.

'No ambulance,' pleaded the wounded man. 'I am a doctor. Please just let me use the phone.' He dialled a number with sticky dexterity. 'Hello, dear,' he said, presumably to his wife. 'I'm afraid I shall be a little late. Someone's just hit me on the head with an axe.'

It was lunchtime in mid-June 1976, just a few days after the first student uprising in Soweto, a date that signified the beginning of the end of apartheid. The racial tension throughout South Africa was almost palpable, particularly in the centre of Johannesburg.

Most of the regulars at the Guildhall bar were gathered on the first floor balcony watching a bizarre and unnerving drama unfolding in the sunlit Library Gardens beneath. A well-built black man had suddenly produced a machete from his windcheater. In the space of ten minutes, he had hacked randomly at half a dozen white passers-by, including the doctor lying bleeding on the bar floor.

Two shots from a traffic officer's .38 brought the axeman down. We were never able to discover the motive for his rampage. Later that same afternoon, according to the police, he 'committed suicide' by hurling himself from a sixth-floor window of police headquarters in John Vorster Square a few blocks away.

Over the years, so many black prisoners had died in the same way at the same building that the ever-cynical Guildhall clientele would allude darkly to the 'John Vorster Square flying club'. They had, after all, chosen to frequent a tavern that was assailed daily by the Johannesburg cacophony of screams, shouts of anger and anguish, gunshots, wailing sirens and triggered burglar alarms.

In those days, the Guildhall upper bar and grill was the favoured watering hole for Johannesburg-based foreign correspondents. It was a convenient stroll from the office building in which most of us rented bureau space. Unlike most of the city's pubs which were tucked in dimly lit basements, the Guildhall was bright and sunny.

It served acceptable lunches in a dining room (the walls of which were dominated, for reasons no one was able to determine, by large portraits of early American presidents). Newspaper accountants in London, New York and elsewhere resigned themselves to fielding large wads of Guildhall accounts from correspondents who, of course, were 'entertaining contacts' on their expenses.

No self-respecting Fleet Street foreign desk was without the Guildhall's telephone numbers, knowing that their man in South Africa would, more often than not, be found there rather than the office. For our part, we could justify those protracted lunches by insisting that we were 'on top of the situation'.

Watching episodes like the 'mad axeman rampage' from the elevated Guildhall balcony, drink in hand of course, helped us maintain this fiction. We overlooked Library Square which became the epicentre of the many demonstrations, strikes and 'rolling mass actions' that characterised South Africa's revolution.

The bombs which exploded in the city centre would rattle the Guildhall's ancient windows but we would sit tight, knowing that a few dazed and bleeding survivors would soon stagger through the door for a liquid shock absorber – and happily unburden themselves of their horror stories.

Word spread that 'upstairs at the Guildhall' was the haunt of foreign journalists. As a result, Bruno's trade was boosted by a procession of proponents, both profane and profound, of myriad causes that they sought to be aired in the international press.

The ensuing debates were always lively, sometimes heated and occasionally violent. Views loudly expressed ranged from the extreme right to the revolutionary left, liberally sprinkled with the pure essence of absurdity that characterises the human condition.

All, irrespective of race, creed, colour or degree of insanity, could be assured of a sympathetic hearing from May, the attractive and imposing barmaid. May's tall, full-figured, invariably charming presence behind the bar was another of the Guildhall's attractions. Her long auburn hair, sparkling green eyes and accent all attested to her professional Irishness.

May not only kept the bar but the peace. She could and would disarm (literally in several cases) potential trouble-makers with her charm and quick wit. She always had an ear and a smile for the problems of the more tired and emotional drinkers.

She was also adept at fielding phone calls from irate wives, girlfriends and news editors: 'He's just left, me darlin' or 'He had a bit too much so I ordered him a taxi' and to London 'Don't fret yourself now. He knows about that story and is on his way to work on it.'

Manny, one of the non-hack regulars, seemed to occupy a corner stool at the bar on a permanent basis. A tall, gaunt, morose figure, Manny was deeply enamoured of May and would glower menacingly at the many customers who flirted with her.

We ascribed his bitterness to the fact that it was unrequited love. Manny tended to be deeply suspicious of all except those from Chingola in Zambia where he was born. He had swallowed a pejorative thesaurus at an early stage. The woes of the world were blamed on the spics, the wops, the wogs, the dagoes, the poms, the yanks, the coolies, the coons, the yids, the polaks'. And, of course, 'the micks', although he obviously made an exception in May's case.

The impending advent of majority rule did little to improve his jaundiced views. An Inkatha rally in Library Square resulted in two very large Zulus, clad in traditional skins and bearing spears, appearing at the Guildhall bar. May ensured that they parked their weapons at the reception desk before serving them with long, cool beers.

A couple of hours later, one of the warriors held the entire pub in thrall with a very good impression of Louis Armstrong. Dabbing his forehead with a white handkerchief and in an impressive, gravelly voice, he went through Old Satchmo's entire repertoire.

The Guildhall clapped and cheered him on, most customers joining in. Even Manny, who had been heard to mutter something about 'bloody Rorke's Drift again' when the Zulus first appeared, attempted to chime in with the chorus of 'What a beautiful world'. Thus did the Guildhall Executive Bar and Grill greet the 'rainbow nation'.

Christopher Munnion was Africa correspondent for the *Daily Telegraph* of London for nearly thirty years. Now a writer and freelance journalist, he lives in Johannesburg.

Alex

John Murphy

The children on Seventh Avenue stop playing and look up, as surprised as if they just saw a meteor drop out of the sky. Could this be right? A van of white tourists is on a Sunday afternoon drive through their black township. This is, after all, Alexandra, a no-go area known for carjackings, killings and cholera. A place so feared by Johannesburg residents that many blacks, let alone whites, don't dare to visit.

But the van stops, and a tour guide steps out along with eight men and women with cameras slung from their shoulders and explains this is the street where Nelson Mandela once lived. The tourists stare at the squalid township shacks, turn up their noses at the smells of raw sewage and tripe sellers and clutch their wallets a little tighter as a crowd gathers.

A skinny township man reeking of beer stumbles towards the group to offer a handshake. 'People think Alexandra is full of murderers and criminals,' he says. 'It's not true. You see?'

It appears the tourists are not convinced of that point. But they are here, and it's enough to assure many residents that not everyone runs from Alexandra. Perhaps some day people from around the world might come for a visit.

That is the dream of a group of business leaders and tour operators who are trying to start a tourism industry in this sprawling, dismal township of more than 700 000 people just north of Johannesburg. The businessmen cite the success of Soweto, South Africa's most famous township, where more than a thousand tourists a day – most of them from the United States and Europe – visit the vibrant community that became synonymous with the struggle against apartheid. Soweto has its share of crime and violence, but tourists are surprised to find it relatively tame. Alexandra is not. And that may be Alexandra's selling point.

'Soweto is too sophisticated,' says Beryl Porter, owner of South Africa Walk Tours, which has started taking tourists into Alexandra once or twice a month. 'Alexandra is a more authentic township. It's the real thing.'

So real that some tour operators hire security guards to escort them through the densely packed streets. Porter's brochure promises the 'Tough world of the squatter. Vibrancy and colour of Pan Africa'. Nervous tourists need not fear. Her 'walking' tour is primarily experienced from the back seat of a van.

The tourists drawn to Alexandra are not from overseas. They are white South Africans who live minutes away in Johannesburg's plush northern suburbs of thatched-roof houses with swimming pools and manicured lawns. Some of the visitors have lived their entire lives within sight of the township but never stepped foot inside its borders.

That's a legacy of the architects of apartheid, who worked diligently to keep the country's races apart. For whites, it's easy to forget the township is there at all. In winter, a thick black haze from coal fires smothers the township. At night, year-around, the township all but disappears because many homes do not have electricity – earning it the nickname 'The Dark City'.

'It's a place you wouldn't go as a white person because of the bad press, the crime, the hijackings,' says Jan Vlaming, a white building contractor from Sandton who never visited Alexandra until he took a Sunday tour. He went now because he was curious.

'There's a move in South Africa to get to know other people,' he says. 'There's a feeling we need to reach out to blacks, Indians and coloureds. If you don't go visit a man where he lives, how can you expect to know what makes him tick?'

Black township residents don't need to ask the same question of whites. Many of Alexandra's residents work as maids, gardeners or construction workers in the spacious homes and glittering shopping malls of the northern suburbs.

When the van turns into Alexandra, the passengers look appalled by the jumble of thousands of tiny shacks. Corrugated metal roofs are weighed down with bricks and stones. 'That's so the roofs won't blow off,' says tour guide Patrick Gumede, an Alexandra resident.

Gumede recites Alexandra's vital statistics: Alexandra is the densest populated area in South Africa, its 700 000 to one million people are crammed into 4.5 square miles. More than half the population is unemployed. Those who do work support families on an average monthly salary of $130. More than seventy per cent of the population is under thirty-five, giving the township the energy and unrest of youth.

H B Papenfus, an unsuccessful farmer who decided to develop his land into a township named after his wife, founded Alexandra in 1912. It was first marketed as a place where blacks and people of mixed race could purchase property, but when apartheid leaders prohibited black land ownership, it filled up with tenant dwellers renting from white landlords. By the 1960s, the area had deteriorated into a slum that became a centre of political protest, including several successful boycotts protesting bus fare increases.

Alexandra was home to many of South Africa's famous musicians and religious and political leaders. When 22-year-old Nelson Mandela moved to Johannesburg from the countryside in 1941, he rented a tiny brick shack with no electricity or running water at 46 Seventh Ave. As a law clerk, Mandela would often walk six miles from Alexandra to his downtown Johannesburg office because he could not afford the bus fare.

'The township was desperately overcrowded; every square foot was occupied either by a ramshackle house or a tin-roofed shack,' Mandela wrote in his autobiography, *Long Walk to Freedom*. 'Life was cheap; the gun and the knife ruled at night.'

The stop at 46 Seventh Ave is a highlight of the tour. No sign marks the home as a historic site. The family living there is sitting down to a lunch of chicken and pap but welcomes the intrusion, inviting the tourists inside.

The van threads its way through the township's narrow streets, alive with shebeens blasting kwaito, and churchgoers and fruit and vegetable sellers. It climbs up into the East Bank, where there is evidence of a government renewal programme started in 1998. The crush of shacks gives way to tidy suburban streets with three-bedroom brick homes, apartment buildings and a park where the Alexandra cricket team squared off against an all-white side from Johannesburg's suburbs.

The look of familiarity drew smiles from the tour.

'If you didn't know this was Alexandra, you wouldn't think it was Alexandra,' comments one surprised South African woman.

'What about crime?' asks another woman. 'I see people hanging clothes outside. If you did that in the northern suburbs, they would disappear.'

'That's because they all come to the northern suburbs to steal,' quips yet another woman.

The last stop is at a bridge overlooking the Jukskei River, which residents continue to use for bathing and washing. Precarious shanties line the riverbank. When the river swells, it often washes away dozens of the homes and their inhabitants.

Vlaming and his wife Morag walk on the bridge and take photo after photo of the grim scene. 'I think it's important that we should see how the others live. It's appalling,' says Morag Vlaming after completing the tour.

And will her neighbours plan a visit? Probably not.

'They are quite happy to live in their cocoon.'

John Murphy is the Africa correspondent for The Baltimore Sun. He lives in Johannesburg.

The Hillbrow haircut

Ravi Nessman

As legend has it, Hillbrow is one of the deepest circles of Dante's hell, a chaotic swirl of prostitutes, drug dealers and murderers that any visitor would be lucky to escape. A post-apocalyptic Wild West that leaves hardened police pale with fear. People might compare it to a war zone, but for one American television reporter's description of it as the most dangerous place in the world that is NOT a war zone.

Which is not to say the myths about Hillbrow aren't true. Crime is outrageous. Sex shops line the streets and the tangy scent of pot drifts over the neighbourhood.

But alongside this, there is life in that dense square kilometre of apartment blocks and shops, a vibrancy and sense of community that is certainly not found in any of Johannesburg's walled-off northern suburbs and sterile malls. Mothers walk outside with their children. Congolese and Nigerian immigrants gather in large groups in the street, talking and gently swaying to music from back home.

Hillbrow is filled with fast food restaurants, pawn shops, music stores, storefront dentists. Vendors sell vegetables off overturned boxes and live chickens from six-foot rolling cages.

And then there are the rows of green tents along the sidewalk, each one a mini-barbershop stocked with nothing but a skilled hand, a plastic chair, an electric razor and some juice to power it.

People work here. People live here.

And I want a haircut.

So for one hour, I will leave my car and wallet behind and venture into Hillbrow.

A South African friend and I took a taxi through its crowded urban streets. He and the driver talked about what the neighbourhood once was and laughed at what it now is: more reminiscent of west Africa, where many of its residents come from, than Johannesburg.

Our driver insisted that the Ponte, the cylindrical high-rise with the neon Vodacom ad rising above the skyline, gave prospective residents a month of free rent, knowing they would flee within days after being robbed or attacked. The story didn't make much sense from a business standpoint, but in the world of Hillbrow legends, it fits right in.

We chose a tent set up in an abandoned lot. On one side was a competing barber. On the other, a makeshift takeout restaurant – a tarp overhead, a table with ceramic dishes and silverware and four coolers filled with meat and cooked corn meal waiting to be dished out for the coming lunch crowd. Across the street, people gathered in small groups talking and laughing. A few were staring.

'Where I come from, people work. Here they just stand around,' Emmanuel the barber said as he tied a smock around my neck.

He is twenty-eight and from Nigeria. He came here three months ago to live with his brother who came three years

195

before. He doesn't live in Hillbrow, just works here. And he hates it, especially the crime, which he blames on Liberian immigrants.

He has been robbed here a few times, most recently of the twenty rand he was carrying as he walked to a pharmacy to buy cold medicine.

'This place is dangerous. There is no order here,' he says. 'There are too many guns.'

He plugs in the electric razor I brought with me in an effort to be hygienic and hesitantly begins giving me a very light trim.

'Don't worry about cutting it too short. I really like it short,' I say.

'OK,' he says, continuing his slow passes through my hair.

A thin man with rolling eyes walked by unsteadily, reeking of pot.

'Caucasian hair is different,' the man says.

No problem, Emmanuel says. He has a few white clients, mainly drug dealers, he says, laughing.

My introduction to Hillbrow came my very first night in Jo'burg, two years ago. I failed to make a crucial turn and instead of meeting a friend for dinner at a shopping mall, I found myself driving past a green sign reading: 'Hillbrow'.

Even as a newcomer to the country, I had heard of Hillbrow, and I knew I did not want to be there. I drove around in circles frantically for a few minutes, straining to read street signs to match them to my map, but too scared to slow down enough to make out the names. I was finally saved by an amused gas station attendant.

Less than two decades ago, Hillbrow was one of the most vibrant neighbourhoods in the city. It was one of the first to desegregate, and the hip and bohemian of all races lived there. It was a land of the trendiest nightclubs and never-ending parties. It was the place all the cool people went on New Year's Eve.

Now, on New Year's Eve, police sit in armoured trucks waiting to squelch the chaos and vandalism that inevitably erupts.

That is Hillbrow at night.

In the daylight, I stare out of Emmanuel's tent at the apartment building across the street. Every balcony has a clothes line filled with fresh washing, a reassuring sign of family. One has a satellite television dish.

Emmanuel smiles as a man puts a cracked plastic chair outside the tent. It is the waiting room, and he has just had it repaired.

Suddenly the power goes out. Like the other vendors, Emmanuel pays a local building superintendent a hundred rand a month to let him snake a long cord down the block and into his building. He runs out to find out what's wrong.

When he comes back, the power is on, but after nearly half an hour, I still have all my hair. Emmanuel complains about the razor I brought.

His partner Kinsley, who has finished a haircut in less than fifteen minutes, says my South African razor is garbage. The one he brought from Nigeria when he moved here over a year ago is the real deal.

'Don't worry, I'm cleaning it,' he says, rubbing alcohol on to a toothbrush and scrubbing his worn razor.

Kinsley takes over, insisting he cut countless white heads when he was a barber in the Ivory Coast. His stay in South Africa is simply the fifth stop on his illegal immigrant's tour of Africa, which has included stays in Liberia and Ghana.

Whether it was his razor or his hand that made the difference is unclear. But in five minutes he was done and handing me a shard of broken mirror to examine the trim.

Nice.

I give them twenty rand, twice the normal price.

I pick up my friend and our driver outside, and we walk back to the taxi unmolested. I tell my friend that Emmanuel and Kinsley both plan to move back to Nigeria soon. They say they can't take it in Hillbrow any more.

He laughs.

'Sure.'

Ravi Nessman is an American journalist based in Johannesburg. He has covered Africa for more than two years.

A house in Ah-frika

Ken Owen

We had a house in Jo'burg. I say that in mocking imitation of Karen Blixen's famous line: 'I had a farm in Ah-frika.' The mockery is intended to hide nostalgia.

Our house was not a farm but it stood on a vast suburban plot thickly covered with trees, part of a landscape that Jo'burgers like to describe as the biggest man-made forest in the world. Ibis squawked morning and evening, and in the green shadows crested barbets peck-peck-pecked at the stump of an old acacia. Outside our bedroom window was an immense tree. We called it a Japanese maple, which it wasn't, but we never did identify it properly. In summer it spread a rich canopy, and in winter it let the sun through. We loved it.

Sheer luck gave us that house. A stockbroker, having listened in disbelief to P W Botha's world-defying 'Rubicon' speech in 1985, packed his Frank Stella paintings and his Mercedes into a container and headed for Sydney. His house, a bit ramshackle but utterly beautiful, was tossed on the market in the middle of a collapse of confidence. We snatched it up, the bargain of our lives.

Those were rough times. Our wealthy suburb, inhabited by whites and their status-conscious servants, lay cheek by jowl with Alexandra, the densely packed slum where the 'comrades' had wrested control from the apartheid government. The police station on the outskirts was heavily sandbagged, and the black policemen had to live with their families in a small, muddy compound of tents, surrounded by razor wire. As 'collaborators' they could not survive otherwise.

Alex was both a different country and a mirror image. When I went there for the funeral of seventeen young activists killed by the police I had to pass through the police station where a white officer gravely wrote down my name and my press card number. Two hundred yards further on, rounding a corner, I was surrounded by young comrades in identical blue T-shirts. They hustled me off to a commissar who gravely wrote down my name and my press card number. Bureaucratic habit survives revolution.

In the nearby soccer stadium were activists, almost comical in their earnest fervour, stomping around, chanting 'Hau! Hau! Hau!' Above, the spectators in the stands waved the forbidden flags of the ANC and, I noted for the first time, the communist hammer and sickle. Winnie Mandela turned up, stylish in proscribed ANC colours.

Here, a mile or two from our pampered neighbourhood where neatly uniformed maids watched the comings and goings to make shrewd assessments of our (and their own) social status, was liberated South Africa.

From our beds, now and again, we heard gunfire from Alex. One night the uproar was so great that I drove, at about 2 am, to see what was happening. I found the entrance to Alex barred by a police car. Beyond lay the dark, mysterious shanties and alleyways, quiet now, but loaded with menace.

'We can't let you go in there,' the policeman said. His job, we both knew, was to preserve apartheid's frontiers, to keep the sleeping white families of our suburb insulated from the rage in Alex, to maintain an illusion of order in a time of disorder. I went back to bed.

More and more, however, disorder was spilling into our suburb. Around the corner, a man was murdered. Further along, in broad daylight, another man was shot and his assailant ran brazenly down the street, pausing only to hide his revolver in a hollow tree. All around us houses were burgled, and people talked of emigrating. The news of each incident, vividly embellished, travelled instantly around the neighbourhood, from gardener to maid and from maid to madam. No detail escaped the watchers. Gradually, as disorder became endemic, the watching faces seemed to become impassive, closed, unfriendly.

Amidst it all, we lived a charmed life. Once the local communists stuffed a letter through my door promising that I would be among the first liberals to face a firing squad after the revolution; later, when Chris Hani was assassinated, my name was found alongside his on a list drawn up by his right-wing killers. My employers sent two men armed with automatic weapons to patrol day and night.

The patrols ruined our lives. The men wandered among the trees, leaned against the Japanese maple, peered into windows. They frightened away the ibis so that I overslept. But when our son screamed in a nightmare, they tumbled into the servants' quarters, slamming the door. 'Somebody's killing those white people in there.' We dispensed with 'security'.

Still we came to no ill. I cannot say why. Only one small incident comes to mind as a possible explanation. During a rather formal dinner party for the sort of people who go to newspaper editors' dinner parties, two maids from next door came diffidently to our door: their gardener had a bone stuck in his throat and might choke to death. I bundled the poor man into my car and drove him to hospital, returning to the table within twenty minutes. I doubt that our guests noticed.

The next day a delegation came to thank me. The maids were there, explaining in wonderment to anybody who would listen that I had come to their aid 'in the middle of a dinner party, so smart'. Suddenly, it seemed to me, the impassive faces were gone from the neighbourhood. People smiled. I smiled. We exchanged polite greetings.

That was all, but as the years passed and the disorder grew, we alone remained untouched. I began to imagine we were living under protection, watched over by some kind of secret neighbourhood network.

No, that's fanciful. Countless whites in Jo'burg have gone out of their way to help black people in distress. It was just luck, and our luck held until liberation and until I retired. The house was sold and the new owners built three more houses on the site, putting a high wall between the bedroom window and the Japanese maple. They made enough money to lure a stockbroker out of Sydney, but the acacia was ripped out and the barbets are gone from our house in Jo'burg, in Ah-frika.

Ken Owen, born in South Africa in 1935, is a former editor of the Sunday Express, Business Day **and the** Sunday Times. **He retired to Cape Town in 1996 in order to fulfil an ambition to sail his own boat across an ocean – which he did.**

Out of Lagos

Barnaby Phillips

Shortly after arriving in this city I sent an email to a friend I'd left behind in Lagos, Nigeria. It read like this . . .

Dear Peter

This is cruel but I can't resist it.

1) I've just moved into my new home. I discovered that the phone line was not working. I called the public phone company, and they came round the next morning and fixed it (the man in the blue overalls did not ask for/hint at/demand a bribe – he just did the work, for free).
2) The Jo'burg newspapers last week complained about 'a petrol shortage crisis'. I nearly wept with laughter. I saw one queue outside a petrol station – it consisted of three cars.
3) Within walking distance of my house is a cashpoint till. I put in

my English bank card, and money comes out.

4) Last week I drove from Johannesburg to Swaziland. It took five minutes to cross the border; no visas required, not even proof that you own your car. My South African mobile phone worked in Swaziland . . .

The list went on. Utterly unremarkable and mundane observations if you are arriving in South Africa from Europe or the United States, or many other parts of the world. But for me, a series of miracles, a succession of revelations, that left me gob-smacked and disoriented. This was not Africa as I knew it and understood it. Not the Africa I'd spent the best part of the previous decade toiling away in; the sweat and heat and corruption and dirt of Lagos, and Luanda and Maputo and all the other cities I had come to know so well. Their turmoil and noise seemed a million miles away, on another continent, from the cold sunny winter of this Johannesburg, where everything worked, where the shops were full of goods, and where all the cars gleamed so new.

We can all do without too much stress in our lives. Anyone who has ever queued for petrol in Nigeria, or pleaded with an Angolan immigration official, or searched for a working telephone in a small town in Mozambique, will agree with me. And months after arriving in Johannesburg, I'm still grateful for all those things that work, still not quite able to believe my luck.

But I'm also more and more aware of what I am missing, of what this city does not offer me. Put simply, it's a sense of engagement, and a sense of belonging. I live in a suburb of high walls and electric fences. I only see my neighbours, and they only see me, when we drive in and out of our automatic garages. They are all white, and English-speaking. At least, I assume they are all English-speaking; in all this time we've barely exchanged more than friendly nods.

The restaurants in my neighbourhood are wonderful; the

food is delicious, the atmosphere mellow. But if there is such a thing as 'a new South Africa', it has not yet happened in these northern suburbs. Those who dine out are almost exclusively white; on the streets the only black people are maids and gardeners. Again, Africa seems so far away; and I don't just mean the breezy cafés of Maputo, where black and white mix freely, the sensual nightclubs of Luanda or the sweaty bars of Freetown and Accra. (In my anodyne suburbia the only nightclubs are in shopping malls.) I also mean the daily contact with people who are battling to overcome poverty and injustice with courage and humour.

Of course, most South Africans are fighting the same odds, and displaying the same qualities – but the apartheid system was designed to keep them as far away as possible. I go to Soweto and Alexandra because I'm a journalist – otherwise, frankly, it would be easy to be ignorant of their very existence. Apartheid's geography still defines this city.

At least, for the time being. Because Johannesburg is changing. The men who built the city turned their back on Africa; but they are long gone, and now Africa is claiming their legacy. In the past decade central Johannesburg has been transformed. White capital has fled, leaving behind vacant tower blocks and empty hotels. It may be fear of crime that drove the whites away, but once the process began, it achieved its own momentum. Perhaps many whites felt uncomfortable as they began to perceive themselves as a minority on streets which had been their exclusive preserve. Whatever, they've taken the real financial and business heart of Johannesburg twenty kilometres to the north, to the shiny new towers of Sandton. And black Africa has moved into the spaces they left behind. The offices downtown are being colonised by small businesses, whilst the streets are bustling with traders, selling fruit, shoes and cheap clothes. To my eyes it looks more like an African city and, in fact, many of these new entrepreneurs do come from as far afield as Nigeria, Congo, Ghana and

Senegal. Listen out for the voices around you; you'll hear Zulu and Xhosa, but also French, Portuguese, Swahili, Wolof and Lingala.

They come from all over, and they are all sorts, the new African migrants. There are the professionals – the doctors and academics, highly educated and hoping that in this country their skills can at last earn them a living wage. There are the traders, buying up what the shopping malls have to offer, and travelling home twice a month with bulging suitcases, knowing they can sell everything at a profit in the markets of Lagos, Kinshasa or Dakar. There are the hawkers and hustlers, who travel south out of desperation, and are willing to turn their hands to anything. And then there are the criminals; the drug dealers, the pimps and fraudsters. (And South Africans, of all colours, will invariably tell you that there are far too many who fit into this category.)

The signs of the African invasion are there, all over the city. From the streets of Yeoville, jostling with Zimbabweans who have fled economic collapse, to the discreet hotels of Illovo and Rivonia, where the corrupt Congolese and Angolan elites come to play, and spend their ill-gotten gains. It's enough to make apartheid's planners turn in their graves. But that's no bad thing.

Barnaby Phillips is a BBC correspondent based in Johannesburg. He has also worked for the BBC in Mozambique, Angola and Nigeria.

Once a Pirate, always a Pirate

Marcus Prior

April 11, 2001. The white sands of the Jolly Harbour resort in Antigua made an odd setting for the news that forty-three South African football fans had been killed in a stampede in a Johannesburg stadium. South Africa's cricketers had just the day before become only the second team in twenty-seven years to win a Test series in the West Indies. Spirits were high. The news jarred terribly.

My mind immediately pitched back twelve years, to another similarly incongruous newsflash. It came inside the pages of Uganda's *Monitor* newspaper – nearly a hundred killed at Hillsborough Stadium in England. I chose to shrug it off as another sloppy misprint (one, maybe, but not one hundred?) until the BBC crackled confirmation over short wave that evening.

There was no avoiding the truth of events at Ellis Park in Johannesburg either, a sporting venue rich with resonance for South Africans. It was there in 1995 that President Nelson Mandela, memorably clad in a Springbok jersey, presented the Rugby World Cup to Francois Pienaar, the blond-haired, blue-eyed personification of Afrikaner manhood. Briefly, a sport that for decades represented little more than apartheid at play united a nation.

Ellis Park is also the leased home ground of one of South Africa's most famous football clubs, Kaizer Chiefs. On April 11 they were hosting bitter local rivals Orlando Pirates – my team.

Allegiances in football are born easily but die hard. My first weekend in Johannesburg included an international athletics meeting at Ellis Park's adjoining stadium and a cricket Test match a few miles up the road, but the centrepiece was my first visit to a Pirates/Chiefs derby at the awesome FNB stadium on the outskirts of Soweto.

The locals have a saying – 'Once a Pirate, always a Pirate'. So it proved, as from that day forward I was a fan of the buccaneers in black and white. It was probably only because friendly strangers on either side repeated the mantra to me throughout the game, but it was reason enough.

South Africans have a habit of underplaying themselves, a tendency to seek modesty when there is genuine reason to boast. The FNB on derby day is one of spectator sport's most compelling occasions – 100 000 fans in a concrete bowl sunk deep into the wastelands of the Rand. Rio de Janeiro's Flu-Fla at the Maracana might have been bigger, but Brazil's greatest derby was dying the same slow death as the country's domestic football. Rangers and Celtic might produce more internecine Glaswegian bile and AC and Inter more Italian sass, but the colour and verve of a Pirates/Chiefs clash are unique. It is something of which South Africans should be proud.

Match day is a calabash of the senses. For a few hours it seems every street trader in town has decamped to the stadium perimeter with an eye on turning a fast profit. Red meat and pap to clog the cleanest artery, T-shirts, key rings, flags and baseball caps all make for brisk business.

If someone approaches and waves a whisky miniature in your face shouting 'cellular' he is not trying to rip you off nor offering you a home-made mobile phone, but peddling an illicit stash of alcohol to smuggle into the stadium. Small enough to be a cellphone, apparently.

On one gloriously comic occasion, a hawker was exposed by a few laddish fans as a trader in ladies' underwear. How he was torn to shreds in a hail of slapstick derision, the plastic bag in which he carried his wares turned inside out, his head daubed with one particularly frilly number while the crowd dissolved into helpless laughter and tried on a few items for themselves. He got his merchandise back, but may have wondered if underwear really was the way ahead.

Unlike my experience of many English football stadiums, the FNB was totally lacking in the thinly veiled threat of violence between fans that so often hangs heavy in the air back home. There was a gunshot on one occasion, but this was Johannesburg after all, and the most violent act I witnessed in several visits over eighteen months was a Chiefs supporter aiming a brick at a Pirates rival. The fact that he was too drunk to throw it more than a couple of feet and that his friends were crying with laughter at his preposterous behaviour defused the confrontation to little more than pantomime.

Perhaps the atmosphere was leavened by the sweet smoke perfume that rises to greet you as you make your way down from the elevated entrances. Puffing through a 'zol' or joint is an acceptable alternative to reading the match programme, but it never seemed to stem the tide of songs, many of them from the mines, which helped keep the struggle against apartheid alive and now serve as football anthems too.

As in so many other parts of the world, but particularly here in Johannesburg, football offers relief from life's interminable grind. It is that more than anything that made the events of April 11 at Ellis Park so tragic.

The cavernous FNB could cope with the organised chaos of a Pirates/Chiefs game. It was becoming increasingly obvious that the plush, modern but significantly smaller Ellis Park could not. Two years earlier we had understood that for ourselves. Holders of valid tickets, we and hundreds of others could not even get into the stadium and instead faced a volley of teargas from nervous riot police. That there was no panic that day was a miracle.

A public inquiry into the Ellis Park disaster pointed the finger at everyone and no one. The blame-game is a futile affair, but at the very least South Africa's football authorities need to ensure the debacle is never repeated. After all, the country is a major contender to host the 2010 World Cup finals.

For those who lost loved ones, a Pirates/Chiefs match will always be a moment of mixed emotions, a day of riotous colour laced with the sorrow of loss.

Life can deal you that hand in Johannesburg.

Marcus Prior is a writer and broadcaster who started his career with the BBC World Service, with whom he moved to Johannesburg in 1998. He is currently in Cape Town as a director of the MWP Media news agency.

Collecting Beggars

Jo-Anne Richards

I have a friend who collects beggars.

It's not a bad hobby for Jo'burg. The butterfly population's way down, unless you drive out to the Magaliesberg. Of course I have been told that other collections are taking off in a big way. The story goes that, dragging Benoni Lake for a missing person, the police amassed three bodies they hadn't even known were missing.

Anyway, my friend now has a sizeable assortment. Her husband says her collection's become so famous that even the blind beggars see her coming.

They come to her door at all times of the day – for money, for old clothes, for food parcels. She's got to know them a little: the old lady who lost her daughter to the big city. What could she do but follow – and hope she might still find her on the street one day. And the sight-impaired man who, mysteriously, sees much better since his bottle-bottom glasses were broken in a fight.

One evening she was out at a drinks party – over Doorn-fontein way where the valley gaped beneath them, toothed by distant mine dumps. She loved coming over this side, out of her northern suburbs refuge into the 'real Joeys'. To the right, the city bowl thrust its brazen light at the encroaching dark. Brash towers jostled for space behind Ponte, whose Vodacom sash flaunted the fact that this was after all a city of trade. Far to the left, cooling towers fumed in some industrial fulmination of their own.

'Aw gee, what a great possie,' they all mooned over the balcony rail in the quirky way local people had of seeing some ethereal beauty of their own in the rough-and-ready jumble of Jo'burg. Despite its view, their host's home was now too close to the city centre to be fashionable. They couldn't sell, their hosts proclaimed. They might as well stay. Worth it though, they felt, when spring came and the jacarandas spread their purple tide as far as you could see.

It was a strange city when you thought about it – constantly redefining itself, shifting its communities and the character of its neighbourhoods. In firm hands it carried its stocks and credits, wheels and deals, the rush of suits and the ring of cellphones. Yet, she felt, it was still large enough in its un-pretentious heart to hold the colours of Shangaan turbans, the bustled trade in saris and silk, the sizzle of street-fried boerewors and the pavement commerce in tomatoes, china dogs and junk. And just fifteen minutes drive, back towards the suburbs she came from, fingers stretched for acrylic extensions, for Earl Grey tea and carrot cake.

My friend stayed longer than she'd intended, caught in the edgy energy that made it seem, at times in this city, that anything were possible – great good and great evil, brilliant successes and abysmal failures. There was a strange urgency to people's partying, as though a natural disaster were to occur in an hour's time, with a lifetime's worth of ardent mingling to fit in before then.

By the time she left, it was quite dark. She played dodgem with taxis while, back in the suburbs, her husband prepared the children for bed. Suddenly, the doorbell rang. Odd, he thought. Who the hell could that be so late?

'Don't go out,' he warned the children. 'I'll check it out through the intercom. Hello? Hello?'

Silence. Must have been a prank – someone passing the electric gate with a yen to bring a little irritation to life in the northern suburbs.

Bing Bong. Bing Bong.

Silence. Jeez, this prankster was persistent.

Bing Bong. Bing Bong. Bing Bong.

'YES. What do you want?'

Tap Tap. Tap Tap. 'UGH UGH UGH UGH.' Tap Tap. Tap Tap.

Jislaaik. Now the guy was making threatening guttural noises and tapping something on the intercom. Could it be a gun? It sounded metallic. Perhaps if he just kept quiet the guy would go away.

Bing Bong. Bing Bong. Bing Bong.

Tap Tap. Tap Tap. 'UGH UGH UGH UGH.' Tap Tap. Tap Tap.

'WHAT THE FUCK DO YOU WANT? LEAVE US ALONE.'

It gave him the creeps, like that urban legend they'd told as kids to scare each other. This guy hears tapping on the roof of his car – Tap Tap. Tap Tap. Eventually he discovers a madman sitting there with his girlfriend's head on a stick.

He pressed the panic button. Within minutes the security company phoned.

'Come quickly,' he said. 'There's some mad guy outside the house trying to scare us. I don't know what his case is, but he could have a gun.'

'The car's on its way, sir. Don't panic. Lock yourselves in the bedroom and don't go out. We'll sort it out.'

My friend's husband huddled in the bedroom with the kids, straining for cars, gunshots, screams ... Oh my God. His wife. How could he not have thought ... she'd be coming home any second. She'd drive right into this mêlée of bodies and blood and ...

With shaking hands he dialled her cellphone. Please let it be on. Please let her not have it somewhere in the rubble on the floor of her car. Please ...

'Hi, I'm nearly home if that's why you're phoning.'

'Where are you?'

'Just opening the gate.'

'Jesus Christ. Don't do that. Can't you see there's some madman out there and he may have a gun. Go. Drive away. Close the gate.'

'Don't be an idiot,' she told him tersely. 'That's not a madman. That's my deaf man. He comes every week.'

At that moment Security descended with a screech of tyres from both directions. The street filled with the pounding of boots and the glint of enormous guns under streetlights. The deaf man looked as though he might die and save them the trouble.

By this time the neighbours had come out to gawk. One or two still clutched bottles of wine so, what the hell, they had a bit of a party. The deaf man was considerably cheered by a quick dop and handouts from slightly drunken neighbours.

The only person who held back was my friend's husband, who felt foolish. Who would have a wife who collected things, he muttered when everyone had stopped laughing. Why couldn't she keep tarantulas? It was a helluva lot less nerve-racking.

The deaf man never came back though. My friend never saw him again. She hopes he is still out there causing terror and mayhem through countless intercoms – and finding at least one person who hears what he's trying to say.

Jo-Anne Richards is a journalist and the author of two novels, *The Innocence of Roast Chicken* and *Touching the Lighthouse*, both published in Johannesburg and London. This story contains descriptive extracts from a newly completed novel about Johannesburg with the working title *Karma City*.

Jozi Quotes

Adam Roberts

City of dreadful night,
of refuge,
of perspiring dreams,
that is set on an hill,
upon a hill,
abstract and premeditated,
big hard-boiled,
rose-red,
splendid,
oppressing,
evil,
this great hive,
without a city wall,
woe to the bloody city,

Hell is a city,
Hell to cities.

For a city consists in men,
the city is not a concrete jungle,
which hath foundations,
it is a human zoo,
of friends,
populous,
of big shoulders,
those streets of the city,
are pure gold,
splendid,
cities we had learned about,
the hum of human cities,
every one,
thou art the flower of cities all,

Hell is a city,
Live in a city.

Adam Roberts is the southern Africa correspondent for *The Economist*. Of British and Swedish parents, he has reported on Africa for four years. He lives in Johannesburg and likes it there.

On the way to work

Arja Salafranca

On the way to work
I see a dead dog on the pavement,
its leg is lifted in rigor mortis,
a meaty chunk of its raw shoulder flesh is exposed.
There are woven baskets for sale
on the opposite side of the road, and round barstools.
The sun burns my driving arm crisp brown.
A desperate woman sells wooden bowls,
comes up to my window. I flick my
eyes away behind mascara-flecked
sunglasses. Her mouth drops a little.
There are men selling bags of avocados
and boxes of green grapes. I say no.

Driving to work I have to detour
around road works through poverty.

The houses are small, shabby, paint peels
and fades away here. Walls are not high,
or non-existent, crumbling. People sit
in their yards and watch the rerouted
traffic bump through the neighbourhood,
observing the unusual event as if it were a parade.
The shops are hot, dark holes. The children amuse
each other by buying sweets, walking,
playing in the streets.
It's a different world here,
a world I've been warned against.

Driving home, one night, a dog leaps
into the dark road. I swerve to avoid its black
jumping shape. It's limping, sick,
frightened or confused.
A group of men stand nearby, laughing
loudly, clustered in groups by their cars.
I put my foot hard down on the petrol pedal,
the dog disappears, defeated,
limping dumbly back from where it came.

Arja Salafranca was born in Spain but has lived in Johannesburg since the age of five. She has published two collections of poems, A Life Stripped of Illusions, winner of the Sanlam Literary Award in 1994, and The Fire in which we Burn. She has published short fiction in a number of local and international journals and anthologies, and received the 1999 Sanlam Award for her short story, 'Couple on the Beach'.

Sophiatown

Anthony Sampson

I first saw Johannesburg in May 1951 when I had just come
to South Africa from London to work for the new *Drum*
magazine. I was driven up from Cape Town for two days along
a thousand miles of sand road, across the half-desert Karoo,
to find the Golden City looking as harsh and hostile as the
Cape was lush and friendly. I stayed in a bleak and beery
hotel in Jeppe Street in the city centre. I could see no river,
park or lake: only patches of brown grass. I thought it was
the end of the world.

But I soon discovered an amazingly creative city, not in
the white suburbs, but in the black slums where the *Drum*
writers and readers lived. In Johannesburg in the early 1950s
there was an explosion of jazz, writing, drama and sport which
seemed like the cultural explosion of Harlem in the 1920s:
the expression of people who were embracing city life with an
energy and optimism which carried its own political message.

The *Drum* office was in downtown Johannesburg, just next to the *Rand Daily Mail*, but it was seen as an alien enclave: visiting white secretaries were astonished to see black men using typewriters, discussing books, even using the same teacups as whites. Few white journalists bothered to visit, but for black writers, politicians and sportsmen it became a social centre as much as a magazine: in the late afternoon the office would fill up with African visitors who would later set off for refreshment at a nearby shebeen.

I felt out of place in white Johannesburg. The more prosperous English-speaking set enjoyed a lifestyle which I had only known from Hollywood movies, in mansions with black servants wearing bandoliers and white gloves who reminded me of *Gone With The Wind*. Many of them had emigrated from England only recently, to escape from post-war Labour austerity; but they seemed to have been transformed by the sun and the servants into a different breed, with much more confidence and fewer doubts.

They seemed like an earlier generation of English, living in streets called Empire Way or Eton Road, retreating to country clubs with immaculate cricket pitches and bowling greens. And they nearly all shared the same views about 'the native' who seemed to have no relationship with the black writers I worked with.

I chose to live in unfashionable Yeoville where I could invite black visitors without attracting notice. But I soon felt more at home in the black townships, in Soweto or Sophiatown, than in most white gatherings. It was Can Themba, the most brilliant of *Drum* writers, who first lured me into the seductive world of Sophiatown, the multiracial slum where he lived in a dingy room which he called 'The House of Truth'. He introduced me to shebeens like Back of the Moon and specially the Thirty Nine Steps, where teachers, gangsters, messengers and politicians were drawn together by illicit liquor. Sophiatown was an impossible place for normal family life, with people jammed up against each other in hovels, sheds or shacks – even in old trams. In many countries it would have been condemned as a dangerous slum, but under an apartheid government it had a special magic as the meeting place for Johannesburgers of all colours, where all the strands could combine to create a multiracial culture and language.

White writers like Alan Paton in *Cry the Beloved Country* described bewildered tribal Africans arriving in Johannesburg, with its bright lights, shiny cars like boxes on wheels and skyscrapers like houses piled on top of each other. But most of the new Johannesburgers I encountered had embraced the big city with gusto, to become more eagerly urbanised than most Afrikaners. The tens of thousands who had arrived during and after the Second World War had to live on their wits or go under, and they faced constant battles – to travel to town, to survive in the streets, to earn extra money or to outwit the police. The more educated newcomers, like Nelson Mandela, Oliver Tambo and Walter Sisulu, still retained their rural roots while they responded to the challenges of the city with constant resourcefulness.

But survival was becoming more difficult, and I had a preview of the full ruthlessness of apartheid when the government decided to demolish the 'black spot' of Sophiatown and to forcibly remove its African inhabitants to Meadowlands, on the edge of Soweto. It was the first major political challenge for the ANC: the walls were scrawled with 'We Won't Move', crowds listened to protest meetings and Nelson Mandela made an explosive speech. Even the cynical Can Themba was infected with the revolutionary spirit, reciting Dickens: 'It was the best of times, the worst of times'. Many Sophiatowners still believed that their spirit could prevail against force. But on the first day of the removals two thousand police arrived in Sophiatown, while the occupants offered no resistance and the workers meekly queued up to take buses to work. Mandela recognised for the first time, as he wrote later, that 'we had no alternative to armed and violent resistance'.

In 1955 I was given my farewell party in Sophiatown, when part of it was already demolished, in a dingy room called the House of Saints. It filled up with the *Drum* writers and local black stars, including the singers Dolly Rathebe and Thandi Klaasen, the guitarist Alpheus Nkosi, the saxophonist Ben Gwigwi. The music started and everyone sprang into jive; the room filled with writhing bodies, the floorboards shook and the lights swayed. The walls seemed to disappear altogether, spirited away by the music and the fast-moving shapes of bodies, legs, or trombone tubes flashing in the light. I would return many times to black Johannesburg over the next half-century: to witness the revolutionary excitement after Sharpeville, the desolation after the Soweto uprising, the euphoria after Mandela's release, the patient voting during the first elections. But I would always remember most vividly the bursting optimism of Johannesburg in the early Fifties. The slums and shacks of Sophiatown disappeared almost half a century ago, but its creativity is still alive in the music, the paintings of Sekoto and the stories of Can Themba.

Anthony Sampson wrote the authorised biography of Nelson Mandela, *Mandela*, and several other books about South Africa. He now lives and works in London.

City Johannesburg

Wally Serote

This way I salute you:
My hand pulses to my back trousers pocket
Or into my inner jacket pocket
For my pass, my life,
Jo'burg City.
My hand like a starved snake rears my pockets
For my thin, ever lean wallet,
While my stomach groans a friendly smile to hunger,
Jo'burg City.
My stomach also devours coppers and papers
Don't you know?
Jo'burg City, I salute you;
When I run out, or roar in a bus to you,
I leave behind me, my love,
My comic houses and people, my dongas and my ever
whirling dust,

My death
That's so related to me as a wink to the eye.
Jo'burg City
I travel on your black and white and roboted roads
Through your thick iron breath that you inhale
At six in the morning and exhale from five noon.
Jo'burg City
That is the time when I come to you,
When your neon flowers flaunt from your electrical
wind,
That is the time when I leave you,
When your neon flowers flaunt their way through the
falling darkness
On your cement trees.
And as I go back, to my love,
My dongas, my dust, my people, my death,
Where death lurks in the dark like a blade in the flesh,
I can feel your roots, anchoring your might, my feebleness
In my flesh, in my mind, in my blood,
And everything about you says it,
That, that is all you need of me.
Jo'burg City, Johannesburg
Listen when I tell you,
There is no fun, nothing, in it,
When you leave the women and men with such frozen
expressions,
Expressions that have tears like furrows of soil erosion,
Jo'burg City, you are dry like death,
Jo'burg City, Johannesburg, Jo'burg City.

Wally Serote works in government and has published several volumes of poetry. 'City Johannesburg' was first published in the book *Yakhal'Inkomo* **in 1972.**

When Orange Farm meets
Sodwana Bay

Mungo Soggot

The survivor of a car hijacking near Johannesburg tells the story of how the gang leader waved his gun and shouted at him in a fury: 'I am a philosophy student . . . I did a degree. I had a job, but I was fired when I had an accident. Do you think I want to do this?'

The victim was an officeholder of the ruling African National Congress, who returned to the country from exile in the early 1990s. He said the five hijackers surrounded his car as he drew up at a friend's house near Orange Farm, an impoverished settlement just south of Johannesburg. One of the hijackers climbed in, struck him on the side of the head with the butt of his revolver, and made him get out. He said he was taken to a nearby shack, forced to drink a bottle of brandy while his assailants cleared the car, and threatened with execution if he did anything silly. He got away, and knows he was lucky. 'They don't just kill whites for nothing – also us blacks.'

One of the wilder myths about Johannesburg is that it is the city's wealthy who bear the brunt of its notorious rate of violent crime. Attacks on plush homes and cars in the city's smart suburbs have a greater chance of making the headlines, but gratuitous violence accompanying robbery is standard fare in the townships and squatter camps surrounding Johannesburg.

The level of frenzied violence in the industrial heartland of South Africa is hardly surprising. Over the past ten years, about a million jobs have been lost nationally. Employment and population statistics are unreliable, but the unemployment rate is generally estimated at between thirty and forty per cent. Go to a place like Orange Farm, which is inhabited mainly by people who cannot afford to live in Soweto, and it is easy to believe the figure is higher. For here, and even in Soweto, the streets teem during the daytime with unemployed men and women. It's the same story across South Africa, but particularly striking in and around Johannesburg, the centre of the economy, and where the jobs are supposed to be. The economy, meanwhile, grows at two per cent – nowhere near the six per cent deemed necessary to reverse the growth in unemployment. With facts like these, as the hijack victim says, what else do you do than turn to crime – often with uncontrollable anger.

Eight years after the collapse of apartheid, many white Johannesburgers remain as unaware of life in the slums and the townships as ever. It is of course the same in many cities with considerable disparities in wealth – a small elite that glides along in parallel to the heaving poverty around it. But in Johannesburg there is a very particular apathy, and a willingness to be blind to reality, that stems directly from the days of apartheid. Most people simply do not want to know.

They first do everything they can to get their money out of the country. Many seek solace in a proliferation of gleaming, first world office and shopping centres that have expanded as the wealthy have moved north, beyond Sandton, getting as far away from the now black business district as possible.

Eight years on, many whites in Johannesburg – as opposed to the rural hinterland – have generally learned not to be overtly racist. Their feelings are complicated, an uncomfortable cocktail of guilt, mistrust and prejudice, but they generally hide them well.

Catch them relaxed and it's a different story. Go to Sodwana Bay, a delightful resort just south of the Mozambique border and a favourite retreat for Joburgers. It's far from any-where – just miraculous beaches, a nature reserve, fine scuba diving, four-wheel-drives, camping and beer. Here you will hear wealthy whites mock blacks' accents to their faces. And you will see young black men, employed by diving companies to ferry the heavy diving equipment, wearing T-shirts with 'slave' emblazoned on them. When asked about it by some astonished Frenchmen, the diving company said it was 'our sense of humour'. And indeed some of the white employees occasionally wear them too. But that doesn't help dilute the image of a portly white man strolling towards his dive boat, while, behind him, a thirteen-year-old black 'slave' lugs his scuba tank.

Perhaps it's the rich sea air on that coast. You would be unsurprised to find this in the untamed Northern Province, but ex Johannesburg? Listen on another weekend to the pre-sentable couple from the southern suburbs in Johannesburg recounting crime stories, and hear the husband talk about how he had wished the black thief had got into his car so he could then shoot him.

With the ever-widening wealth gap, it is likely that crimi-nals will gain ground, growing angrier and more violent. Squatter camps around Johannesburg will mushroom, and the shopping centres will multiply in the rich north. This rough mining town then stands a good chance of becoming an ever-bigger monument to social inequality. The government will continue to implement its business-friendly economic policies, admired in the west and met with bafflement in the townships, which show no signs of propelling the economy anywhere near the level needed to stop the growth in unemployment. The residents of Orange Farm will struggle to pay their taxi fares into town.

To apply the conservative policies, the authorities need to be blinkered themselves. As this time bomb ticks, the crime that has made Johannesburg famous won't need racially inspired hatred to fuel it. Although just imagine what the philosophy student back in Orange Farm does when he gets to hijack one of the four-wheel-drives favoured by the Sodwana Bay brigade.

Mungo Soggot moved from London to Johannesburg in 1994. He worked on *Business Day* and the *Mail & Guardian*, and is now pursuing various freelance projects.

Eyes Wide Open

Veronique Tadjo

It is a sunny day but the sky is of an uneven blue, bright in the middle and muddy at the sides. Is the haze pollution? Trees have a dusty colour, the grass is burnt, yellow.

In the distance, a stream of cars on a highway bridge seems to run silently.

What hopes and disappointments does this city hold?

They came from all parts of the world to dig the soil in search of fortune, to enter the heart of the earth and extract its jewels by all means necessary.

No river runs through her body of steel. Man-made city. No river to lick the dryness of her skin. No lagoon. No lake to adorn her face and make her features softer, gentler, kinder to the inhabitants.

It is a city with a hard look in her eyes, demanding and uncompromising, always asking for more, more . . .

Eyes wide open. Awake, awake, oh, so awake! Never resting

whether in broad daylight or at night.

Man-made city. People rummaging in her inside, at the surface, converging on this land with big dreams of gold, like it has happened before in the times of the Far West in America when the frontier spirit was reigning supreme. And the Eldorado.

'Big dreams are made of this,' say the lyrics of a song. 'Travel the world and the seven seas, everybody is looking for something.'

Jozi – Egoli – The golden city. Why pervert the dream?

The trees that you see were brought when the city was being born. Imported. Planted by the will of men who wanted to settle there because of the richness of the ground under their feet. Today, it is these trees which give Jo'burg a bit of peace, casting their leafy shadows on the hurried pedestrians, shielding whole neighbourhoods from the brightness of the sun.

Who would have thought that this huge city made of glitter and poverty was once a place where wild animals roamed the veld? It was before white settlers came with their all-powerful ambitions to take the land for themselves. That was the epoch when indigenous peoples lived in villages on rock so ancient it may have seen the birth of humanity.

Could it be this mixture between the old and the new which creates a turbulent zone? Like the Indian ocean meeting the Atlantic at the tip of the continent. Warm currents entering cold ones. A whirlpool.

Egoli is over a hundred years old and now millions have converged on her stretch of land, endangering her bloated body. And still more people come every day.

They call it migrant labour. They call it immigration. They call it rural exodus. From Cape Town, Durban, Gaborone, Lusaka, Harare. From the townships to the city. From Limpopo, Mpumalanga and Maputo, newcomers arrive by taxis, trains or on foot. Johannesburg expands, spreading like bushfire.

Planes landing, planes taking off. Europe. West, east, central Africa. America. India, the whole world meeting, shaking the city down to the roots of her foundation.

The energy of these souls passing one another, these bodies colliding, these dreams conflicting, makes a cacophony, an urban music of humming, buzzing, and yelling sounds.

People criss-crossing the crowded streets, everybody going about urgent business matters, as if time was going to end, now, immediately. As if tomorrow was far, too far. Far too uncertain.

Restlessness that takes your breath away and leaves you gasping for a quiet corner in a park, near a fountain or in a square while cars and taxis zoom around.

Look at her high-rise buildings plunging in the sharp sky!

Look at their haughty silhouettes peering far away in the distance towards the sprawling townships! Soweto. Alexandra . . .

The city's heart is broken, her arteries emptied of playfulness. Big money withdrawing, drying out, pouring elsewhere in the northern suburbs. Even the stock exchange has moved.

Paralysis. Immobility. Fear. Don't cover your face, Johannesburg!

And yet every morning, the city carefully dresses herself in many kinds of promises. True or false. Everything is possible. The gates of this once forbidden city, taboo city, have opened for those who were rejected, who were sent back into the night.

Soul shattering to and fro between opulence and depravation, glitter and darkness.

Johannesburg, listen to me, I am trying to find forgiveness.

Your man-made fairy tale was the harsh reality of the injustice I suffered. Of the days when despair was threatening my whole being. The days I also fought with all my heart. A long and painful struggle.

The sun sends sparks of fire in my eyes. You blind me, you

hurt me, Jo'burg, with your incredible stature.

In the quiet suburbs, walls around houses are too high, too hard, making concrete-like cocoons. Neighbours build stronger, larger fences. Remains of bad memories haunt the alleyways.

Egoli walks on a tight rope, searching for a balance between the past and the future.

Why is it then, that she has captured hope, that the future is eating out of her hand? A lot has to be done but so much has already been achieved.

The heart of the city will be reclaimed, the centre made anew, its renaissance shaped by the stubborn spirit of those who have never given up on her, never crossed her out of their lives.

Cantankerous city, what will make you smile again?

Show me your naked face. Show me your warmth and hold out your welcoming arms so I can put my head on your bosom and lay to rest the tormented days.

Somewhere, in an open-air market on a stall, amid eclectic objects and curios, a mask from Mali, its face weary from the long journey, a sacred soul battered, waits for a buyer. Rows and rows of colonial-style, brightly painted statuettes stand to attention with expressionless eyes. Mud cloths, wrappers, traditional cloths tell of another Africa, so close and yet so far, so familiar, yet so foreign.

Veronique Tadjo is a writer, illustrator and painter from Abidjan, Côte d'Ivoire. Her published work includes two collections of poems, three novels, several children's books and a book on Rwanda and its genocide. She lives in Johannesburg with her family.

Johannesburg: Where is your glitter?

Derrick Thema

Just the mention of your name, Johannesburg – the City of Gold – conjured up images of a life of plenty. A life of opportunity and the warm embrace of the skyrocketing buildings that seemed to reach up to the heavens.

Your prim and proper pavements were silhouetted against shop window displays that seemed to endorse your adornment. The scent of the five-star menus that came cascading from your many eateries made it worth our while to be in your proximity. If I could not afford to indulge in your offerings, at least you fed my dreams. One day, one day, I would walk into your belly and partake of your victuals.

My envy built vivid pictures in my mind. I could see myself resplendent in a suit and tie, riding your immaculate elevators. Oh! how wonderful it would be to work on a floor in an office that seemed to welcome dawn with a kiss. The breeze that one would feel in your highest buildings would certainly wash away the unpleasant vibrations spawned by the deprivation of townships like Soweto.

Wasn't I taught that the ways of your custodians were superior and a yardstick by which I should strive?

Oh, I remember that debilitating picture which was in every second house from Sophiatown to Soweto. The picture of our Lord Jesus Christ, juxtaposed against that of Satan. My mind boggled at the fortune of white people. Like most of them, Jesus was white, blond with blue eyes, while Satan was my exact replica – black, fashioned with horns and a pitchfork.

When old black men and women chided us constantly for daring to challenge the omnipotence of white people, they would always remind us that white people are wizards. Look at the aeroplanes. Look at the physical stairs to heaven they have chiselled in their architecture of Jo'burg's skyscrapers. My mind was in turmoil.

Was it a religious decree that those of my ilk who laboured to eke out a living in the hallowed corridors of Jo'burg's buildings earned a pittance? Was it a Christian credo to haunt people of colour by arresting them for not having complied with the many demands of the Influx Control Act that regulated the lives of those who were not white?

While the city was fabled for enhancing one's life, it seemed that only those who dared to go against the stream manifested your dream. Theirs was not a pleasant undertaking. The pick-pockets and handbag snatchers were clearly athletic as, outpacing the law enforcers, they swished down Commissioner and Eloff streets. Those of us who visualised a respectable way to negotiate the Jo'burg dream often saw these acts of desperation as a blight on this wonderful city.

Oh, Jozi! With the gluttony of your custodians to hog all the resources, the dastardly deeds of these muggers and thieves were often visited upon law-abiding citizens.

A trip with parents for a once-a-year shopping spree was the crowning glory of a child's outings. It would, of necessity, herald a stop at a fish and chip shop, a luxury that made the tongue droop with saliva. If lucky, there would be a packet of sweets and perhaps an apple. The aroma of your smarter eateries – we came to accept – was the prerogative of white people.

Your notices, which were everywhere, were a stark reminder of my status as a sojourner. 'Europeans Only' placards constantly kept me in check. Even finding a toilet for 'Non-Europeans' was an act difficult to perform. This weighed heavily on my enthusiasm to visit your sparkling environment; your immediacy became a concrete jungle. Man preyed on man. Your territory became a matter of the survival of the fittest.

And because of the visible presence of law enforcers on your streets, the battle was taken to my turf – the ghetto, the taxi and bus ranks, train stations. The venom of the predators was mostly unleashed on Fridays, when workers were relieved of their meagre wages. There were many casualties. Lives were snuffed out by daggers called 'McGregor'. (The name had nothing to do with the Scots.) Other people were simply thrown out of moving trains. The shoppers who were emptied of their hard-earned cash by confidence tricksters were unknowingly lucky: all they suffered was an emotional and financial setback.

These lonely, prowling beasts impressed many weak-willed people. Were they not the aristocrats? They added a different miasma to your character, Jozi, by swaggering down your streets wearing designer clothes, expensive imported shoes and wide-brimmed hats. At a time when black people were stripped of their land, unable to qualify for bank loans and unable to afford the fancy cars that your custodians cruised around in, the yardstick for prosperity to many black people was underpinned by glossy images. Even factory-worker women developed a tendency to pay for the much sought-after 'Goray' skirt over a period.

Whatever your trappings and weaknesses, you fed the South African dream. You single-handedly prompted the revolt aimed at overturning the exclusivity you represented for white people. But lo! Like a snake in winter hibernation, you have shed your skin: the irony is that it does not glisten any more. The glitter that used to adorn your pavements is no longer there. You cut a forlorn picture of desolation now. Your streets are overrun by the multitudes previously barred from your precincts. The trinkets that once glowed from your shop windows have been replaced by wares that have made your pavements an eyesore.

The areas that used to be your heart and soul – Eloff and Commissioner streets – are now littered with dirt. Some of your once exclusive shops are constantly closed like forsaken orphans. Your buildings are peeling. The steady stream of dreamers is no longer there.

The smell of urine has replaced the sweet aroma that used to flow from your eateries. At a time of abject poverty, where will I turn for a job? Like an amoeba, you have broken into little towns in Rosebank, Sandton, Rivonia and Randburg. Yet the danger once posed in your city centre has seemingly doubled in these supposedly pristine suburbs. Where once a visit to your domain necessitated wearing Sunday best, you are now visited by people who seem to have walked through a bomb blast.

Your healing, Jozi, the heart-throb of Africa, can never be too soon.

Derrick Thema, a journalist, lives and works in Johannesburg. He has published a novel called Kortboy – A Sophiatown Legend and is now writing a biography.

Emily's Story

Jann Turner

'The way people talked about Jo'burg back home, you think that's where I'll go, and I'll get a job there no problem. You really think there's gold there!' Emily Ramorokane laughs rue-fully as she remembers. 'So I came to Jo'burg. But it was hard, really hard.'

For a year the only work she had was on Thursdays, cleaning for an old lady who lived in a suburban retirement village. She was paid twenty rand a day. Half of that went on transport, getting to and from work.

I met Emily in late '96 through my grandmother, who lived in the same retirement village. I had just returned to South Africa from a long stint in the United States, and hired Emily to keep house three days a week. She'd worked in my home for almost four years before I really met her.

One night in February 2000, Emily woke in the blinding light of the beams of torches. Five men ransacked her place and took off with all the things she'd bought in the years since she'd been regularly employed. As they left, one of the thieves grabbed her, dragged her out into the street and raped her. She screamed and fought, but no one came to her rescue.

She came back to work a week later, a shadow of herself. Following counselling at the trauma unit of the Centre for the Study of Violence, she was tested at an STD clinic after complaining of abdominal pain. A week or so later I got a call from her counsellor, who said Emily wanted me to know that she'd been diagnosed HIV positive. It was not the rapist who'd infected her; the test revealed she'd had the virus for some time.

Emily was born thirty-three years ago on the Free State farm where her grandparents and mother laboured. She never knew her father. After attending rural schools until 1983, her family moved to a township outside Bloemfontein. Her high school career was cut short when she fell pregnant at the age of sixteen. 'In our time, when we were at school, they didn't talk much about sex. I was living with my granny and she didn't talk about sex *ever*.' Emily had no idea of the link between intercourse and reproduction. 'I was still stupid, you know!'

So she left school to care for her first child, Martha, whose father absconded before the baby was born. Her second child, Consolation, arrived three years later. Consolation's father was a miner in Welkom, but after a few years he too abandoned Emily. She was forced to leave her kids in the care of her sister and set off to search for work in the City of Gold.

She doesn't think she brought the virus with her. She believes she was infected here, somewhere in the melting pot of Johannesburg. She has had less than a dozen sexual partners in her life, but she doesn't care to know which one infected her with HIV. She's more concerned with staying alive.

Two years ago it didn't look like she'd live much longer. She was a part-time employee with a pension but no medical aid. Her only option was the public hospital system, which would not provide anti-retrovirals but could offer treatment for the opportunistic infections caused by HIV/Aids. Emily's counsellor had heard that Hillbrow Clinic might provide more, but on investigation we discovered that all Hillbrow could offer was counselling, basic treatment for opportunistic infections and, if you were lucky, you might get on to a clinical trial. A number of doctors were involved in clinical trials of new anti-retroviral drugs, but by definition these trials were potluck: you could get a placebo, or you might get on a trial lasting eighteen months, after which you had nothing.

So we decided to investigate the private route. Emily went to Kenridge Hospital for a CD4 count test, an investigation revealing the extent of the viral load. (An ordinary person has a CD4 count in the range of 600 to 800. Clinically, a person is diagnosed as having Aids as opposed to HIV infection when their CD4 count goes below 200.) Emily's was 52. It meant she had been living with the virus for a very long time, and had developed full blown, asymptomatic Aids.

Doctors told Emily her only chance was to go on the cocktail of anti-retrovirals, costing around R4 500 a month. It was impossible.

Extensive research eventually revealed an affordable medical aid scheme that would offer her benefits three months later. Luckily, Emily squeaked in, the waiting period being extended to a year not long after she enrolled. Once on medical aid, she was eligible for a managed health care programme based on the principle that it is cheaper to give Aids sufferers anti-retroviral treatment and prevent them getting illnesses than it is to let them get sick.

In October 2000, Emily started taking the drug cocktail. She changed her lifestyle and eating habits. Two years on, she's healthier than ever.

When I asked her recently what she thought about the controversy surrounding President Thabo Mbeki, who had questioned whether HIV causes Aids, she said: 'I can say the President is trying all his best.' What is his message? 'His message is be faithful to your partner, always use a condom and if you feel that you don't want to have sex, just stay on your own.' And what about the question of whether or not HIV causes Aids? 'OK, in my understanding HIV can't cause Aids if you are faithful to the partner you have. But that's confusing because those people who don't have the medication get diseases that are Aids. If you can't get good medication and healthy foods, eating fruits and vegetables when you are HIV positive, then you will get Aids.'

Last year Emily's sister died from heart failure. After Christmas, Emily brought her two nieces and her own two daughters to live with her in Johannesburg. 'I used to be sometimes lonely when I was on my own. Now I've got my kids, I laugh all the time. I don't want a boyfriend. I don't think I've got any connection with men.' Emily and her four children live together in a flat in a secure complex in Bertrams, near the centre of town. 'It's very safe, very nice. We have a community now; we have a club where we make birthdays for the kids. It's very nice.'

The other day we celebrated Emily's birthday with a cake and cool drinks at lunchtime. We were joined by a group of workmen who were at the house to tile the stoep. They sang happy birthday in an assortment of our official languages and when they'd finished, Emily gave me a hug and said quietly: 'I made it. Another year.'

Jann Turner is a resident of Melville, Johannesburg: the last place on earth she ever imagined she'd be and the only place she'd like to live right now. She's the author of three novels – *Heartland* and *The Southern Cross* and *Home is where you find it*. Emily Ramorokane agreed that her story could be published.

Take your body where it has never been before

Marlene van Niekerk

In the nowhere city which is Jo'burg we, the people of the leisured classes, always seem to be taking our bodies to where they've been before.

Along the bleak, billboard-encrusted thoroughfares of this city we take them to safe places, walled or otherwise enclosed, exclusive, places which provide the flattering illusion of meaningful being and dwelling. We travel in our burglar-proof cars from our walled and wired houses to the well-patrolled labyrinths of Westgate, Eastgate, Northgate, all those lookalike bunker-faced shopping malls. Or, if we consider ourselves too cool for trolleys, we take our bods out to some leafy suburb, to a carefully preserved villagey street, where we cling to our tables in cutesy coffee bars or linger in second-hand bookshops before they disappear, like countless others before them, into even safer neighbourhoods.

We'll follow them there too and protect them all over again for as long as they last, sipping our sidewalk cappuccinos, sheltering behind our newspapers and our cellphones. And so we try to shut out the beggars and the parking attendants gesturing to us endlessly from the margins of our guarded field of vision.

There is no 'there' in the nowhere city. Gertrude Stein's comment about the American urban dystopias hold for Johannesburg too, a city that for its own economic and political reasons increasingly lacks a natural and organic centre with its own irresistible magnetism for an indwelling community. And so, in this sprawling placeless place where glittering affluence and abject wretchedness are chained together like dead and living bodies, we are always en route, we always have places to go.

The urban health club is one of these places, guarded and exclusive like all our favourite destinations. But it promises, in pulsating neon writing, something entirely unique, a chance to take our bodies where they've never been before. We suspend our disbelief and we keep on going back, again and again, to take our bodies to that where.

Reading the phenomenon of the modern urban gymnasium is an exercise in complicit critique. The institution does not reveal itself fully to those who have not participated in it in a literally heartfelt way, and a critique is therefore both a confession and an act of myth-making. Only sworn accomplices can absolve one through their understanding and supportive testimony. And perhaps some little grace may be harvested from this – the grace of community, albeit the uneasy kind of community whose members can smirk at their own myth while upholding it religiously.

Between those regular members of the health club who have come to share a pittance of social consciousness, a moment of mutual recognition might be exchanged on entering through the turnstiles or on inserting the body into the machines of the toning circuit: we are here for life! Or on leaving, passing out through the glass doors, greeting the guard and staying upwind of the vagrants, filled with gratified exhaustion, a towel slung around the neck like a wreath of wilted laurel, their eyes might meet furtively to admit: we've had our fix, a habit through which we shield ourselves, a slight protective veneer that has to be reapplied, preferably every day, like an anti-death deodorant.

The health club privatises social spacing and upholds its own forms of exclusion and subtle oppression. This is a community that collectively retreats into generalised conformity and a shared resentment of strangers and oddballs – such as the dwarf and his assistant who came in one night, or the sado-masochistic couple in search of public thrills, whose deviant behaviour didn't go down too well among the regulars. The space of the gym is designed to provide relief from the gaze of the hungry, encountered at almost every red traffic light on the way there. It provides an asylum and a cure for those suffering from the indifference that has come to be known as 'compassion fatigue'. In the gym they can celebrate their indifference in a safely structured and sanctioned way.

Perhaps the gym here keeps open a protean space, a distorted and painfully aberrant offspring of the parks in European metropolises, of the traditional marketplaces in African towns, where more or less the same people regularly converge for semi-public, semi-intimate togetherness. Here is a seminal form of the multicultural bonhomie prematurely dubbed, by politicians and pop stars alike, 'the rainbow nation'.

But some things could only happen in this South African space.

One evening I spotted a strange visitor, a redundant body, left over from an era when weightlifting had nothing to do with fitness and everything to do with wily skills and a metaphysical quarrel with gravity.

He had a fierce neck, covered in permanently distended veins and tendons, betraying some uncontrolled habit of straining. The effect was very like that produced by the carefully monitored exertions of the regular bodybuilder. Mumbling excuses, swaggering extravagantly, he bustled his way to the free-weight section. Here, with a great sense of purpose, he selected several flat, round weights. Then he lay down on his stomach and motioned someone to come and stack them on his back. He started to do push-ups, shuddering violently, embarrassing everybody, implying with his behaviour that there is a world where notions of 'burden', 'feat', 'struggle' and 'trick' still involve solid and resistant entities.

I went up to him after his workout where he hung over the balustrade, gaunt with some incredibly old-fashioned sorrow.

'You don't come to the gym often,' I ventured.

He looked at me with the childlike candour that some rough men of old still possess and readily confessed. He had the blues. He needed to pull some weights. He used to be a horse-lifter with Boswell & Wilkie's circus, in a wrestling suit with tiger-stripes and black leather leggings laced up to the knee. But then the SPCA complained.

He used to lift a horse hanging in a harness, backstepping up a suspended rope ladder, the horse hanging from a leather strap over his right shoulder.

'That was more than lifting a weight,' he said. That was about balance and timing, I gathered, and about whispering sweet nothings to an airborne horse, pleading for self-induced lightness, for slow, regular horsebreaths. That was about having an accomplice with delicate ears conspiring with one against the deadly pull of the sawdusted earth below.

'That kept me humble,' he said, 'although I was a hero. There were trumpets and spotlights and rounds of applause. When I got down I mounted her and she carried me in a trot around the ring. I deserved that. And so did she. Why should horses always carry men? And not the other way around? It happened just where we're standing now, when this was still an empty lot. The tent used to be pitched right here where they came and built the gym.'

Marlene van Niekerk is the author of collections of poetry and short stories. She wrote the novel *Triomf*, in Afrikaans. It tells the story of four people who live in the suburb built on the ruins of old Sophiatown, once the vibrant centre of black Johannesburg.

I saw a man spinning

Sahm Venter

Whenever we drove around that corner I thought of the spinning man. We always took that route on a Saturday afternoon – the quickest way home. Conversation in the old blue jalopy stopped just as we turned into the road that ran alongside the cemetery. The engine would slow slightly as if to observe a measure of respect. We didn't look to our right, but out of the corners of our eyes we saw the rows of grey headstones appear in the gaps of tree trunks. Out of the corners of our hearts we saw beyond the magnificent sixty-year-old pines into a pain we could not express.

No one ever spoke of our silence, our shared memory. But we all knew what it meant. To speak of what happened that day and the impact it had on all of us would have broken our hearts all over again.

West Park Cemetery is Johannesburg's elite graveyard, where some 200 000 former residents of the city are buried.

Established three years before the National Party came to power and unleashed its insanity on the country, West Park is a model of separateness. Even though the city by-laws allowed any Johannesburg resident to be buried there, it was mainly white residents who came to rest.

Its divisions are largely religious. A bit, a very big bit, for Dutch Reformed Church worshippers. A place for Jews. Another section for Anglicans. One for Roman Catholics which is divided again: priests and nuns, Polish and Belgians. There's a Chinese section, a small part for Muslims and a new one for Hindus. War veterans and police have their own separate areas. A whole section is devoted to 'Westdene', for the scores of white children killed when their school bus hurtled down a hill and plunged into the Westdene Dam.

As a child growing up in Jo'burg, I thought West Park Cemetery was a place for grannies and grandpas. A place where you see grown men crying the kind of tears reserved for times when someone old goes to heaven. Sad tears. But not the kind of wrenching grief born of a life taken too soon.

Thulani was born into a new South Africa. A new country, full of promise. A country which wanted us to mourn equally for every life lost.

It was 1998 and he had just seen his first birthday. A second child after his ten-year-old brother, Thulani seemed always to be ill. In and out of hospital. But a joy to his parents. The frequent trips to the hospital were to them just part of looking after a boy with a better future.

But one night in October Thulani became very ill and the ambulance was summoned. The little bundle wrapped in his father's arms made another journey to the hospital. He didn't come back.

A certificate said Thulani was dead. His heart had stopped beating after only twelve months and sixteen days.

'What did they say?'

Barely a whisper made it out of the strong man's body.

'HIV.'

He pushed forward a piece of paper, the death certificate.

'Where do you want to bury him?' It had to be asked. The tiny soul was being fetched from the hospital mortuary to lie alone in the funeral parlour.

'Alexandra.' A black cemetery in a black township. 'Why not West Park? It's much nearer.'

'But it's for whites.'

South Africa, the free, independent country was less than five years old, but the vestiges of apartheid had a long life left to roam through the psyches of those who had survived it.

That is how we came to be driving along D F Malan Drive. Daniel Francois Malan, a man who would live longer than his life. The road leading to the cemetery was renamed for Beyers Naude, a heroic Johannesburg man, an Afrikaner who bucked the system and fought for non-racialism and democracy. But it was the ghost of Daniel Malan which hovered that day as a small group of mourners drove through the gates and along the edge to the 'Baby Section'.

The tiny white coffin holding Thulani's body was to be laid to rest at the end of a line of buried babies. All kinds of babies, all colours, all faiths, all causes of death.

We stood with the priest near the freshly dug hole. A bird screeched above our community of grief. 'Look down,' she seemed to urge. Below on the ground, inches away from our feet, lay the fragile shell encasing her unhatched baby. We moved aside, watching Thulani's coffin.

With the final words of prayer, Thulani's father stepped into the grave to help the men in brown overalls treat his son with dignity. Arms outstretched, he waited in the red earth for the white box. Carefully he placed it in the ground.

Then it happened. As if he had been struck by an invisible force, Thulani's father spun around in the grave. We gasped. But he continued, silently, never losing his balance. Then he climbed out of his son's grave in a much-changed world. A world where black babies could be buried alongside white. But it was too late for celebration.

Sahm Venter was born in Johannesburg and has been a journalist for twenty-one years. She has worked for both South African and foreign media in print, radio and television. This is a true story.

The Mural

Ivan Vladislavić

I

Not long after Marilyn and I came to live in Blenheim Street, new people moved into the house at No. 10. And not long after that, they employed a woman to paint a Ndebele design on their garden wall. As I was passing by one morning, I saw her marking out the pattern with a felt-tip pen on the white surface, and, over the following days, I went up the road regularly to watch her progress. When she had finished the pattern, an immense maze of black lines, six or seven metres long and two metres high, she began to fill it in with paint – mainly blue and green, if memory serves me correctly. She used little tins of Plascon, the standard household enamel, and ordinary brushes of the kind you can buy at the hardware store.

There was a fad for Ndebele painting at the time. A woman

called Esther Mahlangu had been commissioned to coat a BMW 525 in Ndebele colours as part of an advertising campaign. Or was it an art project? Either way, it was a striking symbolic moment in the invention of the new South Africa: a supposedly traditional, indigenous culture laying claim to one of the most desirable products our consumer culture had to offer, smoothly wrapping this contemporary symbol of status, wealth and sophisticated style in its colours. Perhaps this same woman had wound up here in Kensington? No, I decided, Mahlangu's saloon had been seen all around the world, she had made a name for herself. She would surely have moved on to commissions larger and grander than garden walls – churches, convention centres, hotel dining rooms, the lobbies of health and racquet clubs.

My friend Liz said the whole Ndebele fad was kitsch. It was like that braai sauce people sloshed over everything to give it an African flavour. Tomatoes and onions and too much chilli. Someone just made it up.

But that's how culture evolves, I said. People make things up. Who's to say what will be regarded as 'authentic' a generation from now? Why shouldn't we have Ndebele patterns on suburban walls? What if the people living there happen to be Ndebele? Anyway, only someone with a custodial view of African culture would regard as 'traditional' an art form that arose so recently. Ndebele wall painting is no more than a few decades old, it's constantly changing, and it's full of contemporary references. We were standing on the pavement outside No. 10 as we spoke, and so I could refer to the bright new mural in support of my point. This funnel shape here, which looks like a geometric abstraction, is actually a stylised light. One of those cheap industrial light-shades you'd see in a factory or a servant's room. Once you know that, you'll realise that the little dab of yellow at the bottom is a light bulb. Charming, don't you think? And this shape here, which looks like a bow tie, is derived from a sweet. A boiled sweet in a plastic wrapper.

Liz was impressed with my analysis (which I'd found in a magazine article about Esther Mahlangu, to tell the truth), but sceptical about the mural. It's so cheerful, she said, it makes me want to spit. Like a kiddie's colouring book, with nothing outside the lines. That's why you whites like it so much. Nice and tidy.

I thought it was bravely optimistic. It suited the early Nineties perfectly: Africa was coming to the suburbs in the nicest possible way. I grew to love that wall. My only fear was that some racist would deface it. I could already see the insulting graffiti, dripping bile. But no one ever laid a finger on it.

Long afterwards, it occurred to me that I might have documented the making of the mural. It would have made a wonderful photographic essay. Or even better, a film. That intricate pattern, vibrant and complex as stained glass – it was no child's drawing, never mind what Liz said – spreading out, segment by segment, over a blank white wall. What a metaphor for the social transformation we were living through!

If only you were a film maker, Marilyn said, or a photographer.

But I'm a writer, for Pete's sake, I could have spoken to the painter. I should have got her name, at least. I'm walking around with my eyes wide open, taking everything in like a vacuum cleaner, coughing bits of it out on paper. But I never bother to get the facts.

II

On the pavement outside No. 10 Blenheim: a tall man whose splattered overall and abstracted demeanour spoke of long experience in house-painting. He had spread a strip of plastic at the foot of the garden wall, beneath our Ndebele mural, and was stirring a tin of paint with a stick. The mural must have been two or three years old by then. He's touching up the cracks, I told myself hopefully, although it was obvious what he was really doing. As I drew near, he laid the stick across the top of the tin and went to stand on the other side of the street. Like a woodsman sizing up a tree, just before he chopped it down.

I couldn't watch. I went on to the Gem to fetch the paper. Coming home, I nearly made a detour along Albemarle Street to avoid the scene entirely, but it had to be faced.

He had started on the left. He was hacking into the pattern, obliterating it with extravagant swipes of the roller. Standing back, from time to time, to admire his handiwork. As if there was anything to be seen but an act of vandalism. The man must be a brute, I thought. It would be a man, too, the very antithesis of the woman who had painted the mural. I tried to remember her, but she had faded in my memory. I saw a middle-aged woman with a blanket knotted about her, wearing neck rings and a beaded headdress – but this was Esther Mahlangu, the painter of the BMW, whose photograph had been in the newspapers many times! In any event, they were not opposites. She was not an artist and he was not a vandal. They were simply people employed by the owners of a suburban house to perform a task. What the one had been employed to do, the other had now been employed to undo.

It was unthinkable that the same person could have commanded both tasks. The house had been on the market for some time, and my theory was that it had finally changed hands. The new owner was remaking the place in his own style. Ndebele murals are an acquired taste, after all.

My brother Branko had a less charitable interpretation. They haven't found a buyer, he said, and it's no bloody wonder. They're finally taking the estate agent's advice: paint it white. It's a dictum. Matches every lounge suite.

However, they did not paint it white. They painted it a

lemony yellow with green trim, a petrol-station colour scheme. It took a couple of coats: after the first one, you could still see the African geometry developing, like a Polaroid image, as the paint dried.

Having missed the opportunity to document the birth of the mural through a lack of foresight, I now lacked the inclination to document its demise. This would make a wonderful film, I said to myself. But I did not call my friends the film makers. I did not rush home to fetch a camera. I did not even take out a pad and pencil like a cub reporter. I just stood on the other side of the street and watched for a while, as the design vanished stroke by stroke, and then I went home with a heavy heart.

III

I am stripping the bedroom door down to the wood. The paint comes off in layers: layers of taste, of personal preference, of style. I wish I could read these strata the way a forester reads the rings of a felled tree, deciphering the lean seasons, the years of plenty, the catastrophes, the triumphs. Instead, I see nothing but fashion. Nineties ochre, Eighties ivory, Seventies beige, Sixties olive. Paging back into the past.

I am reminded of the Ndebele mural up the road. It is still there, of course, under a thick, lemon-yellow skin. All summer, after every storm, I have been waiting for it to reappear through the paint, its black edges and angles coming to light again like an old master's pentimenti. But apparently Plascon on plaster does not behave like oil on canvas. To effect this revelation, one would need some paint stripper, a blowlamp, a sharp-edged scraper. Or one of those X-ray cameras they use to hurry on the work of time.

There is an easier way, I suppose. Someone must have photographed that wall. *Style* magazine or the local rag. A dozen kids from the youth hostel around the corner.

But I do not want a photograph.

Sunday morning. The new owner of the house with the secret mural – or perhaps he is just a tenant – is coming down Blenheim Street as I am going up. He is wearing rubber sandals with reptilian soles, satin running shorts, a pair of narrow sunglasses curved like the front end of an expensive car. Under his arm, a folded newspaper; dangling from his hand, a plastic bag full of groceries, the aroma of freshly baked rolls. He slips the bag over his wrist as he unlocks his security gate. I want to tell him what he's missing. I can see myself drawing him back on to the pavement, I can see him gazing at his yellow wall with new eyes. I want to describe the mural, and the man who painted over it.

But I cannot picture this man clearly any more. His work of obliteration hardly took a weekend, and so I couldn't have seen him more than two or three times in all. Now he has vanished behind an impostor. The man I've written down here, the tall one in the overalls, has displaced the one who might have been loitering in my memory. Every time the memory man tries to come from the shadows, this written man, this invention you've already met, steps in front of him. Like a naughty child in a photograph, jumping in front of his meeker brother to annoy him, waving his arms, bullying him out of the picture.

Now who's to say whether this painter, this tall man in overalls, was even tall, was even wearing overalls? And who's to say what was in his mind as he finished stirring his paint and stepped back to look at the wall?

A 'pentimento', in the jargon of art historians, is a place where the painter 'repented' or changed his mind, revealed with the passage of time as the concealing paint ages and becomes transparent. In her book *Pentimento*, Lillian Hellman took this process as a metaphor for the writing of a memoir. The appearance of the original conception and the second thought, superimposed within the same frame, is 'a way of seeing and then seeing again'.

There is something to be said for falling back on the fallible memory, the way one falls back on a soft bed at the end of a working day.

This is the version of the painter I will persevere with: he is a sensitive man, not a butcher. It pains him that he has to wipe out this mural, which reminds him of his own past. When he stands in the glow of these colours, he feels the light of childhood on his skin. But he is a pragmatist too, and has to put food on his table. He steps back to look at the wall, to get the whole thing clear in his mind, to let it settle on the damp soil of his memory. He knows that he is the last person who will ever see it like this. Then he takes up his roller and gets on with the job.

Ivan Vladislavić is a writer and editor. His most recent novel, The Restless Supermarket, is a portrait of Johannesburg in transition. He co-edited the volume blank__Architecture, apartheid and after with Hilton Judin. The three pieces published here are part of an ongoing series of texts about Johannesburg and first appeared in a longer sequence titled 'An accidental island', in David Goldblatt: Fifty One Years.

Acknowledgements

The editors gratefully acknowledge the following persons for permission to reproduce copyright material in *From Jo'burg to Jozi*:

Phalane Motale, *Sunday Sun*, for 'Jo'burg idolised and scorned' by Andrew Molefe and for 'The Master of English' by Johnny Masilela;

Jonathan Ball Publishers (Pty) Ltd for 'City Johannesburg' by Mongane Wally Serote;

Ivan Vladislavić for 'The Mural';

NAI Uitgewers for 'Take your body where it has never been before' by Marlene van Niekerk;

Kgafela oa Magogodi for 'aftertears' from *Thy Condom Come*;

University of Natal Press for the extract from *Welcome To Our Hillbrow* by Phaswane Mpe;

Lionel Abrahams for 'Thoughts on Johannesburg's Centenary';

The Daily Telegraph for 'Jo'burg Lovesong' by Rian Malan;

The *Mail & Guardian* for 'Tatty whore with a heart of gold' by Bongani Madondo.